COMIC BOOK BABYLON
A CAUTIONARY TALE OF SEX, DRUGS & COMICS

TIM PILCHER

TWO BUN PRESS

Published by
Two Bun Press
Copyright © 2013 Tim PIlcher

A catalogue record for this book is available for the British Library

ISBN 978-0-9927339-1-9 (Paperback)
ISBN 978-0-9927339-0-2 (Hardback)
ISBN 978-0-9927339-3-3 (eBook - ePub)
ISBN 978-0-9927339-2-6 (eBook - Kindle)

Edited by Pádraig Ó Méalóid & Brad Brooks
Final Copyedit by Liz Brooks
Cover and icon design by Rian Hughes @ Device
Interior design & typesetting by Brad Brooks @ Grafica by the Sea
Typeset in Minion Pro, Steed Condensed Heavy & Tungsten Medium

Printed by UKComics

CONTENTS

ACKNOWLEDGEMENTS

This book is a memoir. That is to say, it's highly likely not be historically accurate in *any* aspect. Memory can play funny tricks. Gore Vidal once wrote, "A memoir is how one remembers one's own life, while an autobiography is history, requiring research, dates and facts double-checked." While I've attempted to do the latter as much as possible, there's also every possibility that many of the events and people in here are entirely fictional, and any resemblance to real people, alive or dead, is purely coincidental. As Neil Gaiman said in *American Gods*, "I can believe things that are true and things that aren't true, and I can believe things where nobody knows if they're true or not." The scenarios in here may have taken place in a different order or sequence of events, or not at all, as I fall victim to False Memory Syndrome. Hence, the original title was going to be *A Life Less Sequential*.

There's an old adage that "If you can remember [insert event here] you weren't really there." Well, I can remember very little about the Vertigo London Office days. Certainly, blame can be placed at the doorstep of certain "lifestyle choices" for burning out key recall neurons. So I'd like to thank the following people (in no particular order) for plugging my memory gaps with recollections of their own: Angelos, Philip Bond, Brad and Liz Brooks, Al Davidson, Glyn Dillon, Garth Ennis, David Hine, Peter Hogan, John McCrea, John McSweeny, Joseph Melchior, Stuart Moore, Grant Morrison, Peter Rubenstein, Andrew Stickland, Steve White, Alan Martin, and Hassan Yussuf.

Thanks to Brad Brooks and Pádraig Ó Méalóid for their proofing skills and valuable feedback. Any technical, factual or grammatical errors are mine alone. They tried to warn me, but I foolish brushed away their concerns. A massive "Cheer!" also to Brad for his laying out and typesetting of the book.

Huge thanks to Rian Hughes for the fantastic cover design. You, sir, are the finest design guru I know (apart from Brad, of course)!

Dedicated to all the comic book friends I've lost over the years: Colin Fawcett, Tom Frame, Archie Goodwin, Neal Pozner, Andy Roberts, Martin Skidmore, Lou Stathis, and Steve Whittaker.

Massive thanks to Sue, Megan, Oskar, Bunsen, and Scuttley for putting up with my derelictions of duty and workaholicism. Also to my dad, who inspired my love for comics and desire to be a writer, and to my mum, for not throwing out my comic collection. She left me to do that.

Tim Pilcher
Brighton, October 2013

PRELUDE

"Oh my God. Oh wow. Everything's all full of light. It's beautiful. This is the most amazing thing. I can't stop talking." That's the girl's reaction when she first takes Ecstasy in Grant Morrison and Philip Bond's 1995 comic, *Kill Your Boyfriend*.

My own initial experience with the drug, in a small basement flat in Paddington, was not dissimilarly inarticulate, "Oh fuckin' hell. Shit. That's so—Fuck. Ha! I can't believe it." Et cetera. It was an evening that opened up my eyes to an alternate universe. A universe of infinite colours and possibilities. I was seeing patterns on the walls. The low level lights sparkled and twinkled, as if through a starlight filter. I looked at my friends, Art, Paul and Ellie, and tribal tattoos were appearing on their faces and arms. Intricate swirling patterns that morphed and changed.

I was smiling. I couldn't stop smiling. I was smiling so hard it hurt. I wanted to strip off and dance and shout. I had a deep, overwhelming love for everyone in the room. Not just for being my friends, or for introducing me to this new reality. Not even because they'd allowed me into their inner circle, but simply because they were fellow human beings, made of the same beautiful light as I was.

We stayed up till sunrise, talking, dancing, sensing, while the MDMA worked its magic on our synapses. This was fantastic. I was on top of the world and embraced in an all-encompassing, unconditional love. I had entered a living comic book world, where anything was possible.

It would never get that good again.

CHAPTER ONE
DESCRIPTION OF THE WRITER AS A YOUNG MAN

"I can tread on the heels of his memories, see through his child's eyes and feel the early blossoming of his self-awareness."

—**Millennium Fever**, Nick Abadzis & Duncan Fegredo

My dad held me tightly by the hand as he strode through a crowded, noisy, smelly London fruit 'n' veg street market. The road was littered with banana boxes, discarded orange tissue wrappers and abandoned grapes. My little legs struggled to keep pace with his determined stride, while simultaneously trying to dodge through the labyrinthine crowd. His long, dark, Seventies-style hair blew in the summer breeze, as I looked up at his Zapata-moustachioed face. Where we were going, I didn't know, but when we got there, there was a hushed reverence about the place.

The shop was a rag-tag mess of piles of magazines, stacks of Hawkwind albums, musty old science fiction paperbacks and bins of bargain basement comics. Various hairy, young men shuffled about the place rummaging through the endless publications, panning for gold. The place reeked of patchouli oil, presumably to mask the mustiness of old paper and poor personal hygiene.

The most impressive thing there was a huge wooden cut-out figure of Captain America by Jack Kirby on the wall, just above the stairs to the basement. His dynamic pose, leaping towards the viewer in the bright red, white and blue of the costume, as he brandished his giant shield, seared itself into my brain. From then on I was hooked on comics. I was five years old. The shop was Dark They Were and Golden Eyed.

To non-comic fans it's hard to describe how important Dark They Were and Golden Eyed was to the modern British comics industry. This was where it all began. It was the first proto-comic shop in the UK. British Comics Fandom had its roots here.

Mike Lake and Nick Landau met here and formed the legendary conflicted powerhouse duo that would set up the Forbidden Planet retail chain, Titan Distribution and Titan Books publishing house. Paul Hudson worked here and would go on to run three successful Comic Showcase shops in London, Cambridge and Oxford. Josh Palmano used to visit here and eventually set up his famous Gosh! Comics—possibly the best loved comic shop in London today. It was the clubhouse of what were to become some of the most influential comic creators the UK ever produced. Brian Bolland, Dave Gibbons, Alan Moore and Bryan Talbot all hung out here. As did Marvel UK and *Warrior* founder Dez Skinn. And a teenage mod-haired, leather-jacketed Neil Gaiman would frequently pop in, before heading off down the road to catch the latest bands at The Marquee, whenever he got into London. This was the nexus point. Genesis. Ground Zero. THE BIG BANG. In musical terms, Dark They Were… was the Sex Pistols playing at the Manchester Free Trade Hall on 4 June 1976.

Dark They Were… was run by Derek "Bram" Stokes and took its convoluted name from a Ray Bradbury short story. Some kids' dads take them religiously to football matches every Saturday and inspire a life-long tribal loyalty to the sport. My dad was different. For the few brief years we lived at the Toc H men's hostel in Fitzroy Square, London, every Saturday morning, he would take me down to Dark They Were… I'd check out the comic bins, while he'd look through the endless science fiction paperbacks, like Michael Moorcock's Elric series and William Tenn's *Of Men and Monsters*. The latter had a profound effect on me as a child, with its evocative cover of a tribal man with a spear fighting a giant crab-like creature, painted by supreme fantasy artist, Boris Vallejo.

Unbeknownst to me at the time, upstairs was also the first semi-official offices of *The Fortean Times* where Bob Rickard, Paul

Sieveking and Steve Moore would meet "every Tuesday afternoon", to discuss everything from Spontaneous Human Combustion to frogs found alive inside sealed stones. Steve Moore also wrote comics and would become a mentor to his namesake, Alan.

This small proto-comic shop was where I was spiritually born.

After several years of moving around between London, Cornwall, and Kent, my parents finally settled in Virginia Water, on the Surrey/Berkshire border. My mum was employed as a live-in housekeeper and we had a large house to ourselves, next to an even larger house that she had to cook for, clean and manage. I was seven.

The first comics I consciously remember wanting and buying with my own money weren't the *Beano* and *Dandy* (I was already a member of the former's Dennis the Menace fan club, with its furry, goggle-eyed Gnasher badge). I was more cutting edge than that. My best friend, Andrew, and I both read *Krazy*. Launched by IPC in October 1976, *Krazy* was a humour comic that had a more contemporary, anti-establishment feel to it than anything the distinctly conservative Dundee-based DC Thomson published. We were entering the age of punk, after all. The back cover was always disguised as something innocuous like a schoolbook, a newspaper or some highbrow literature, so it could be flipped over at a moment's notice, whenever a parent or teacher strolled by. The lead story was the *Krazy Gang*, featuring Cheeky, and their battles with their nemesis, the fetid Pongo Snodgrass. I loved it with a passion.

The mid- to late-Seventies was a fantastic boom time for British comics. In the space of four years, four publications were launched that were to change my life and inform my comics reading for the next 20 years. I was into the new wave of edgy comics being put out by writer/editor Pat Mills and his cohorts at IPC. Those titles were *Battle*, *Action*, *Starlord* and *2000 AD*. 1975's *Battle* was a war comic and—along with *Commando Picture Library*—taught me all the German I'd ever need to know, from "Achtung!" "Schell!" and "Donner und Blitzen" to "Gott im Himmel!" and "Nien! Nien! Der Englander Schwien!" However, unlike DC Thomson's *Commando* series, *Battle* was brutal in its depictions of war. *Darkie's Mob*—apart from having unfortunately unintentional racist connotations in its title—was a savage story of WWII in South East Asia. One issue saw the eponymous hero nailed to a corrugated steel roof by the Japanese, in all its bloody glory.

And *Action* wasn't much better. Here, we had possibly the most subversive comic of the Seventies. Issue #1 was cover-dated Valentine's Day, 1976 and it massacred the competition. The comic lifted concepts—or "dead cribs" as Mills called them—from all the cool films that were out at the time and turned them into strips for kids. *Jaws* became *Hook Jaw*, *Rollerball* became *Death Game 1999* and *Dirty Harry* became *Dredger*. It was a masterstroke. All these were films I, and my friends, wanted to see, but were far too young to get into at the cinema. But now I could get my own versions on the comics' page, for a mere 7p! Every story was bloody, violent and subversive.

The very gore and brutality that made *Action* popular with me and all the other kids, also acted as a red flag to "concerned citizens", with *The Sun* newspaper calling it "the seven penny nightmare". *Action* became the centre of a campaign led by do-gooding busybody Mary Whitehouse and her evil cronies, the National Viewers' and Listeners' Association, as they tried to ban the comic. IPC sensed trouble on the wind and tried toning the content down.

By September 1976—less than seven months after launching— they even sent *Action*'s editor, John Sanders, on to the primetime TV show *Nationwide*, where he tried to defend the comic from a forceful attack by interviewer Frank Bough, who condemned the comic for corrupting Britain's youth. This was the same Frank Bough who was later vilified in the tabloids in the '90s for taking cocaine, wearing lingerie at sex parties and visiting dominatrixes. Nothing wrong with any of that, of course, but if the tabloids have taught us anything, it's that self-righteousness is a double-edged weapon that's dangerous for those in the public eye to wield.

Bough's fall from grace paradoxically happened around the same time as Martin Barker's excellent book *Action – The Story of a Violent Comic* was released. History loves irony.

Although *Action* remained popular, its days were numbered and it eventually was watered down so much that it was merged with *Battle* to create *Battle Action*, before the *Action* part was finally removed.

However, creator Pat Mills learnt a lot from creating *Action* and put all this knowledge into his next opus. When *2000 AD* launched on 26th February 1977, punk rock was flourishing and the magazine borrowed liberally from the culture, with characters like Spikes Harvey Rotten. The comic was a revelation to an eight-year-old me. Mature, radical and unusual, it became my favourite comic after *Action* had its balls cut off by the media. Although, admittedly, it was initially all about the free gifts. Prog 1 (they didn't call them issues) came with a cheap red plastic mini-Frisbee or "Space Spinner" as they called it. My friend Andrew and I bought multiple copies of Prog 2 to get the *M.A.C.H. 1* stickers. *M.A.C.H. 1* was a *Six Million Dollar Man* rip-off—sorry, "dead crib". The TV series was the hottest show around and one of our favourites. The stickers depicted bits of wiring and electronics you were supposed to put on your body "revealing" your bionics underneath. I recall being in a restaurant with Andrew's parents and us, bored, covering our arms in fake digital circuitry. Incidentally, Andrew had on his bedroom wall a similar cut-out of Captain America I'd first seen in Dark They Were. Only this image was taken from the cover of *Captain America* #193 (January, 1976) by Jack Kirby and John Romita Snr. I coveted that almost life-size wooden figure for years.

2000 AD was "edited" by Tharg, a green alien with a telephone dial ("The Rosette of Sirius") stuck on his forehead, who apparently had nothing better to do than mess around with Earth's periodical publishing industry. "Borag Thungg, Earthlets" he greeted us, introducing a generation of boys to a new "Zarjaz" language. The rest of the editorial and creative staff were all robots with names like Burt (Richard Burton—not the actor), AALN-1 (Alan Grant), Mac-2 (Alan Mackenzie), Bish-OP (David Bishop) and Dig-L (Andy Diggle). It was a bit of a crap in-joke, but we went along for the ride anyway, our tongues firmly planted in our cheeks. It's a daft joke that *2000 AD* insists on pursuing to this day.

I also remember buying multiple copies of *Starlord* #1. In May 1978 I traded the free "badges" of fictional space regiments, (actually shiny metallic stickers), in a desperate attempt at getting the complete set, with fellow pupils at St. Jude's Middle School, Englefield Green. My favourite story was the horrific *Planet of the Damned*, written by Pat Mills under the pseudonym of R.E. Wright and drawn by a succession of Spanish artists. *Planet...* saw a group of survivors from a plane crash that had crossed through some dimensional portal in the Bermuda Triangle and ended up on a deadly planet where practically everything—animals, plants, rain—tried to maim, kill, or eat the survivors' faces off. It had a profound effect on me, to the point that nearly all my creative writing in my English classes was devoted to grim survival stories. I actually preferred *Starlord* to *2000 AD*. It was darker, more dangerous and grisly. But I was in the minority. Sales were suffering and so it succumbed to the savage law of IPC—which had also spelt the death of *Action*: "Hatch, Match and Dispatch." That meant: Hatch a new title; Match it with a new similar title; then Dispatch the weaker selling title by merging it with the bigger hit. Often this would come with a "health warning" on the cover stating "Attention readers: Exciting news inside!" A sure indicator that the comic was doomed.

When *Starlord* merged with *2000 AD*—and eventually died, just five months later—it bequeathed its best characters to its successor: Strontium Dog, AKA Johnny Alpha, and the brilliantly named robots Ro-Jaws and Hammerstein (whose excellent pun I'm afraid I didn't pick up on until at least a decade later) went on to be huge hits in *2000 AD*.

2000 AD introduced me to some of the best British comics creators the country had ever produced. It was a golden era of creativity. I studied the art of Steve Dillon and Garry Leach. Their composition, pacing, body language and facial expressions brought everything they drew to life. Of course, I loved Brian Bolland's work on Judge Dredd, but his work had a stiffness and solidity that Leach and Dillon had managed to shrug off. I endlessly traced and copied their work, in some futile belief that I would crack the secret of their skill and, in turn, magically be able to draw equally as well. When Dillon spent the entire summer of 1983 drawing the epic Judge Dredd saga, *Cry of the Werewolf*, I couldn't have been happier.

Out of all the comics from my youth, *2000 AD* was the one constant in my life from the age of seven until I was 21. For 14 years it was my companion through puberty and into adulthood. In the early years I used to produce my own "radio plays"—which were essentially me reading out the various parts from *Harry 20 on the High Rock*, in different voices and recorded on tape cassettes. Thankfully none of these exist anymore.

Perhaps unsurprisingly, I was regarded as somewhat of a nerd at school. I unwittingly set myself up as a target by taking a large black briefcase to school and openly confessing to playing *Dungeons & Dragons*. I spent my secondary school days on the verge of beatings, only just managing to use my gift of the gab to avoid the bruises. Being a comic fan didn't help. But every Saturday made the week a little more bearable, and it could never come round fast enough, as I escaped into a fantasy world of future lawmen, cowboys rounding up dinosaurs and giant, killer polar bears.

Pretty soon comics, in any shape or form, permeated my entire life. Being an only child, they were my escape from a humdrum existence. They were my friends. They were how I marked time. While on a fortnight's holiday with my parents in Tunisia—a cheap and popular package holiday destination in the late Seventies—I managed to buy and read every single *Battle Picture Library* war comic I could find in the local shop. I even resorted to buying the French-language comics anthology, *Pif*. Admittedly it did come with a free gift—which could make square boiled eggs—that had caught my eye. I came back with a stuffed lizard, after my parents refused to buy me a live chameleon from a street vendor. I also returned with an interest in Francophone comics.

Our long-since-vanished local library in Virginia Water supplied me with all the *Tintin* and *Asterix* "albums" I could gorge myself on. But it also opened my world up to lesser-known French translations such as *Asterix* creators René Goscinny and Albert Uderzo's *Oumpah-pah* and Goscinny and Jean Tabary's *Iznogoud* series. I voraciously guzzled it all, my literary gluttony knowing no bounds. I was a graphic gourmand whose eyes consumed these visual repasts with a passion. Thus, my ongoing desire for Bande Dessinée (French comic books) was kindled.

I was 13 when my parents, their friends, and I all took off for the Capital Radio Jazz Festival on Sunday 18 July 1982. We drove up in two cars to Knebworth Park on a blazing hot summer's day and the line-up included The Crusaders, Dizzy Gillespie and Spyro Gyra. Ingrate that I was, all I really remember doing is visiting the stalls where I managed to pick up some Titan Book collections of classic *Judge Dredd* reprints from *2000 AD* (*The Cursed Earth* Part 1 and *Judge Death*, with fabulous art by Brian Bolland). There was also a big, old, psychedelically painted, London double-decker bus promoting a weird, arty comic magazine called *pssst!* I took a sneaky look at it. It had strips by artists like Paul Johnson, Glenn Dakin and Bryan Talbot that were practically impossible for me to decipher. The whole thing was all very avant-garde and neither the art nor the stories grabbed me in any way, but then, I wasn't the target audience. However, it was on this very bus that a very nice, thin, young man with glasses called Paul Gravett, had spent the previous miserable winter touring the UK, promoting *pssst!* to a disinterested public. While our paths just missed here, they would cross many times in the years to come.

Whenever my mum would do the weekly shop at the supermarket in Egham, I would visit the newsagent's next door. This was an incredible Aladdin's cave of wonders. This enormous member of the Martin's chain stocked just about every conceivable periodical in existence, including many titles that were unavailable anywhere else. They had all the standard American DC (Not to be confused with the Dundee-based DC Thomson) and Marvel superhero comics, of course, like *The X-Men* or *Justice League of America*, but it was here that I discovered my maturing tastes in comics—I'd come some way since being confused by *pssst!* I came across the lavish, full-colour, thick, magazine-sized *Epic Illustrated*, published by Marvel and edited by the late Archie "Nicest guy in comics" Goodwin. The high page count and production values were reflected in the price and it reminded me of my dad's copies of the science-based *Omni* magazine. Reading Rick Veitch's *Abraxas and The Earthman* for the first time, in those pages, blew my tiny teenaged mind. This "*Moby Dick* in Space" was unlike anything I'd ever experienced. Where else could you read about the crew of a spaceship who consisted of a giant praying mantis, a half-woman/half-leopard and an Earthman who wore his own flayed skin like a wrap? The ship itself looked like a giant tree, as it glided through the galaxy in search of a giant, red space-whale—the Abraxas of the title. Psychedelic comics at their best, it was simultaneously engrossing and unsettling, and I remained frustrated that I'd have to wait a whole month for the next issue (I'd been spoilt by *2000 AD*'s weekly schedule).

Within that newsagent's I also discovered Marvel UK's *Captain Britain*, written by Jamie Delano and drawn by Alan Davis. I was a huge Alan Davis fan at the time, right from his early work on the aforementioned *Harry Twenty on the High Rock* in *2000 AD*. The earlier episodes of *Captain Britain* by Alan's Moore and Davis that appeared in *Mighty World of Marvel* and *Daredevils*, slipped under my usually acute comics radar. In fact, the vast majority of Marvel UK's output—with the exception of the initial launch of *Captain Britain Weekly* by Chris Claremont and Herb Trimpe in 1976—completely slid past me, like some Teflon-coated stealth publisher.

But it was in this newsagents, this wonderful purveyor of dreams, that I first discovered possibly the most important British comic launched since *2000 AD*, *Warrior*. Similarly, I'd managed to miss this black and white magazine-sized anthology for four whole months, but as soon as I saw issue #5, I was hooked.

I ordered the first four issues in the post from a man called Dez Skinn, who was the editor/publisher. Three whole months passed, and I'd all but given up hope of ever filling the gaps in my collection when they arrived. This meant I could now catch up on the missing chapters of my favourite strips, *Marvelman* by Alan Moore and Garry Leach, and *V for Vendetta*, by Moore and drawn by David Lloyd.

Warrior was a portal to a world of comics I was completely unaware of. The cover to issue #1 proclaimed "He's Back! Axel Pressbutton-The Psychotic Cyborg!" I didn't even know who he was, let alone that he'd been away. Similarly, the *Marvelman* strip had the hero announcing, "I'm back!" But the sheer presumption and audacity that I should know who these characters were carried me on. I eventually discovered that Axel Pressbutton had appeared in a strip, *The Stars My Degradation* written by Steve Moore and drawn by Alan Moore (under the guises of Pedro Henry and Curt Vile) for *Sounds* music magazine, whereas *Marvelman* was a British superhero created by Mick Anglo 15 years before I was born. Both were completely esoteric to me, but it actually didn't matter what their origins were, as they'd been completely revamped for *Warrior*.

I loved the fact that on the back covers of *Warrior* they had a catalogue of all the cool badges you could buy. Twenty years later I would work with Dez on his *Comics International* magazine, and other projects, and the whole experience was enlightening and highly educational. Apparently, the designs on the back cover were the actual ones used to make the badges. All Dez was doing was running off a couple of extra hundred covers from the printers and using those to make the badges in a typical money saving Skinn scam—you can take the man out of Yorkshire, but…

Years later my parents became friends with Lis Massey, who, it turned out, used to work on *Warrior* as Editorial and PR Assistant, and posed for the cover of #13 by Garry Leach. My dad shares the same birthday as Lis. I only mention that to illustrate how small the world is and how it was fated that my life was to be entwined with comics.

After all, comics were undoubtedly in my blood from day one. I had "four colour funnies" running through my veins before I'd even heard the expression. Cut me and I bled cyan, magenta, yellow and black. I inhaled the musty smell of old comics, as if they were perfume. I sweated Indian ink and I came in process white. It was my destiny to work in comics.

At least that's what I told myself as I folded a purple-striped business shirt and put it back on the shelf for the fourth time that day, fighting back the mind-numbing tedium that gnawed at the back of my brain. I had spent the best part of a year working in Austin Reed's menswear shop in "The Royal Borough of Windsor" and was slowly being driven insane by the banality and poor dress sense of local businessmen. I had started working there on Saturdays while at Windsor & Maidenhead Art College studying "Design & Display" in the misguided belief that this was a graphic design course. It turned out that it was, in fact, window dressing, and I was the only guy on the course. The only thing that I did of any note there was to make a replica of *V for Vendetta*'s Guy Fawkes-inspired mask—based on the cover painting by Garry Leach on the cover of *Warrior* #11. This was 25 years before the Anonymous "hacktivists" and the Occupy movement adopted the image and made it a ubiquitous *bête noire*. After six months of less-than-enthusiastic input from me, the art college asked me to "shape up or ship out." I chose the latter, and rashly took up a full-time position at Windsor's premier men's outfitters.

There is something inherently creepy about men's suit retailers, and Austin Reed's was no exception. For those that have ever seen

The Fast Show's "Suits you, Sir!" sketches, it was *exactly* like that. Paul Whitehouse's character even looked like my manager, Barry.

My time at Austin Reed's was tedious beyond belief. We once had a promo video installed with a TV screen in our department and we were unable to turn the sound down. Thus, we were subjected to the same musical loop every 15 minutes, eight hours a day, five days a week, for over a month. Even now, if I hear *Captain of Her Heart* by Double, or Bill Withers' *Lovely Day* I have a Pavlovian compulsion to smash the nearest television set. The only highlights of the Austin Reed days were a schoolboy crush on my 50-year-old co-worker, Carol (I had a thing for older women), and serving TV presenter, Johnny Ball.

He was getting ready to do a new series of his famous maths/science programmes; *Think of a Number*; *Think Again…*; *Think of a Title With the Word Think in It*, etc. He was a lovely bloke, but had absolutely no dress sense. He needed a series of tie and shirts for the show and I helped show him which ties matched with which shirts. It was a mild joy switching on the TV and seeing him wearing the clothes I'd sold him, and more importantly, in the right combinations. When I remarked this to his daughter, Zoe, years later at an awards do, she jokingly agreed that her dad's dress sense was cause of much consternation in the Ball household.

Having left home aged 16, I was trapped, living in the only accommodation I could afford—a bedsit room in a grotty building in the salubrious sounding Eton. The reality was a shithole. I had one room in which to live, that had the following furniture:

1 wonky wardrobe

1 single, lumpy bed

1 brown, stained chest of drawers

2 chairs (a small, rickety wooden one and a slightly larger, musty armchair)

1 table on which sat a tiny, ancient, rusting Belling cooker, which had a hot plate and a grill.

All this filled the entire room, with a tiny space to be able to shuffle from the bed to the armchair. The shared bathroom across the hall had a stark, foreboding metal bowl, which doubled as kitchen sink and washbasin. There were no curtains in the room and indeterminate stains in the bath.

In the next room was a mentally unstable, heavily homemade-tattooed ex-squaddie who played loud music all night through the paper-thin walls. I once recklessly complained, receiving only threats and the volume increasing for my bother. To compound my woes, the landlord was a fat, miserable cunt of a man, with a terrible comb-over (as if there is any other sort), who would demand his rent, in cash, on the dot, every month. I suspect he wasn't paying taxes. Worse, his personal hygiene and sartorial elegance were woefully lacking.

I would work from 8:30am till 6pm, walk home and sustain myself on beans on toast, pot noodles or similar derivates, while, less than half a mile up the road, Etonian students were dining on *foie gras* and peasants. The only thing that made this particularly grim period of my life bearable in bedsit land was my passion for comics.

Every Monday, on my day off, I would scour the newsagents of Windsor for my weekly fix of comic books. The reason for this was that:

a. There were no local comic shops.

b. I couldn't afford to go to the London comic shops every week, and

c. The inequities of comic book distribution in the UK.

Until the early 1990s American comics were distributed into British newsagents by Comag. However, their policies were less than discriminating and were seemingly based on bulk, rather than consistency of titles. This meant that while one newsagent might've got in *Captain Atom*, *ElfQuest*, *JLA* and *Batman and the Outsiders* one week, another would've got *Wonder Woman*, *Blue Beetle* and *X-Men*. The following month this could be switched around, or completely different titles would appear. Consequently, in order for me to get my weekly fix of comics, I had to trawl across town to at least four different newsagents to ensure I didn't miss an issue of my favourite titles. Having said that, back then I was pretty undiscerning—picking up practically anything, provided it had a logo on the cover with a circle with four stars on it surrounding the two big initials: D and C.

As a kid, DC Comics always spoke to me in a way that Marvel never did. Whether it was the characters, the writing, the art, or a combination of all three, I got something from that company that Marvel's titles could never quite satisfy. In the UK there was a famous kid's humour comic called *Whizzer & Chips*. The idea was that it was, in fact, "Two comics in one, double the fun!" You were either a "Whizz-Kid" or a "Chip-ite." In Scottish football, you're either a Rangers or a Celtic fan. For New Yorkers, it's either Mets or Yankees. And for American comics… you were either a Marvel fan or a DC fan. I fell hard, and irrevocably, into the latter camp.

It was during these grim days of living in Eton that I first discovered Alan Moore's tenure, already halfway through, on DC's *Swamp Thing*. Mixed amongst the brightly coloured spandex titles and flashy superheroic gaudiness, *Swamp Thing* stood out with its inverted palette of muted greens, browns and blues, and dark, heavily inked and brooding fully painted covers. This was something different. Something special. And very possibly something dangerous. I was hooked. These tales of menstruating werewolves, sub-aquatic vampires and terrors too terrible to tell, kept me awake at night. It never occurred to me that this writer was the same one who had wowed me just a few years earlier with *D.R. & Quinch* in *2000 AD* and *V for Vendetta* in *Warrior*.

In 1986 I started saving my money for monthly trips up to the London comic shops to get the precious gems I couldn't find locally—back issues of titles I'd missed and those titles that never made it out to the newsagents. My two regular haunts were Forbidden Planet (FP) on Denmark Street and the Virgin Megastore concessionary, round the corner on Oxford Street. The former had replaced Dark They Were… as *the* comic book Mecca for fanboys. It was the first comic shop proper, set up by Mike Lake and Nick Landau in 1978. A more disparate pair you could not meet. Mike was your archetypal laid-back hippie stoner; long, dark hair and denim. Whereas Nick was the cutthroat businessman; glasses, short hair and sharp suits, with a penchant for fast cars. Yet, together they managed to inspire the explosion in comic book retailing in the capital and beyond.

FP's bags, ads and T-shirts featured a wonderful drawing by Brian Bolland featuring a menagerie of assorted, scary mutants, freaks and weirdoes staring right back at the viewer. A knobbly-headed creature was saying "People like us shop at…" and underneath ran "Forbidden Planet." It was a powerful icon—welcoming readers into a gang of oddballs and outcasts—that became associated with the shop for many years, before they switched to the current rocket logo, designed by *en font terrible*, Rian Hughes. Planet was not dissimilar to Dark They Were…, in that there was a slightly more organised chaotic mess. There was a bagging desk in the middle of the shop, which was where I first met Win Wiacek (who had previously worked at Dez Skinn's Quality Comics shop). But as a shop, FP was dark and slightly foreboding.

By contrast, the small concession stand in the Virgin Megastore was retina-blindingly bright, with spotlights burning down, like miniature suns, on customer and staff alike, making the place a sweatbox in the summer. The tiny shop was hidden up a single flight of stairs within the Megastore, and was not the sort of place you stumbled upon. You had to know where you were going, and why. I first met Mike O'Donaghue (better known as MOD) here, as he worked behind the back issues racks that circled the entire shop, separating the customers from the staff, like some paper-based fortress. MOD went on to establish one of the earliest, more progressive comic shops at the time, Meanwhile… in Camden Town. That was around the corner from my third regular venue, Mega-City Comics.

I can still recall the vicarious thrill of picking up *Watchmen* #11 at Virgin and being stunned, unable to wait for the conclusion of Moore and Gibbons' ground-breaking opus, but having to! Those long train journeys back to Eton flew by as I voraciously devoured my new "post-literate" booty.

It was on one of these buying trips that I first heard about a comic convention happening at the end of the year. I was nervous about heading up to London on my own for a whole weekend, but I finally plucked up enough courage and cash and headed up to the "Smoke" one weekend in October 1986 for the second UKCAC.

For the uninitiated, I should explain. As the comic book business was booming at that time, three smart chaps, Frank Plowright, Hassan Yusuf and Andrew Littlefield (and later Richard Barker), started up a convention for the growing legions of comic fans who wanted to gather together, eat crisps and talk about a subject that no one else in their lives gave a toss about. Unfortunately, Messrs Plowright, Yussaf and Barker decided to call the annual gathering the United Kingdom Comic Art Convention. That's UKCAC for short.

That's, *you cack*. The name was a constant source of amusement, with many booklet sketches commenting:

"UKCAC?"
"No."
"It must've been me then."

UKCAC was, by no means, the first British comic convention, there had been intermittent ones since 1976, but it was *my* first. The con was a revelation. Here were hundreds of people, just like me! Comic fans, unashamed in their passion. I was no longer a lone voice in the wilderness. Although, at the time, I knew no one at that particular show, in the "Fandom Assembled" list in the booklet there are 58 people who would eventually become my friends, co-workers, business colleagues, bosses, and flatmates. People like Duncan Fegredo and Matt Brooker, who had yet to break into comics professionally were just as wide-eyed and hopeful as me. That year the guests included Alan Davis and Dave Gibbons, who provided the booklet cover of Superman battling Thor. Others who attended were Gil Kane, Garry Leach, David Lloyd, Alan Moore, Frank Miller and Bill Sienkiewicz. Karen Berger was also there, acting as DC Comics' British Liaison, seeking out up-and-coming talent. At that point I had no idea who she was, but she would play a pivotal role in my life seven years later.

There were comics quizzes, art classes and all manner of panels. I remember a mind-blowing Brendan McCarthy art exhibition, and he has remained one of my favourite artists ever since.

I got my booklet signed by *2000 AD* "script droid" Alan Grant, US writer of *Batman* Mike W. Barr, artists Jim Baikie, Brian Bolland, John Bolton, Brett Ewins and many more.

I was 17 and was too poor to afford the subsidised lodgings in the student halls of residence, arranged by the convention, let alone a hotel, so I spent the night at the all-night cinema screening, trying desperately to sleep on three rickety plastic chairs in a huge, parquet-floored chilly gym hall at the University of London Union. The intensely eclectic film selection (long before the days of the "comic book movie" explosion) included *Dune*, *Zelig*, *Crimes of Passion* and *Revenge of the Nerds*—a tenuous, if not vaguely insulting, link to sequential art at best. After a rough night of trying to sleep through *1941* and *Body Double* I emerged with a crick in my neck and a sniffly nose.

Comics were going through a renaissance. A brief, short-lived one, as it turned out, but one that caught enough of the public's imagination none the less. Suddenly in every magazine and newspaper there were articles about, and interviews with, Alan Moore and Frank Miller. The *Daily Mail*'s Sunday supplement, *You Magazine*, even put *The Dark Knight Returns* on the cover of its 2 November 1986 issue, with a four-page article inside. A young journalist called Neil Gaiman wrote a piece on *Watchmen* for the now defunct *Today* newspaper.

But the majority of newspaper articles around that first attempt for comics to gain respectability featured immature headlines like "Biff! Baff! Pow! Comics Grow Up!" These became so prevalent that they became a cliché in comics circles and were a testament to the distinct lack of imagination of newspaper and magazine sub-editors.

Similarly, whenever you switched the TV on there was another dodgy documentary talking about the new wave of serious adult comics; all illustrated by terrible sound effects and puerile sub-Sixties *Batman* TV series graphics, that only highlighted that the production company had completely missed the point. Yet again.

Alongside *The Dark Knight* and *Watchmen*, Art Spiegelman's *Maus* was elevated as proof of comics' new-found maturity. These three graphic novels (despite all being serialised elsewhere and the press being completely uninterested then) formed a "Holy Trinity" that was exulted by the media for almost a decade. It was just a shame that the industry didn't back them up until the 21st Century.

But despite the mishandling of the subject matter, the point was that comics were getting the column inches and airtime previously denied them for so long. The genie was out of the bottle.

I started visiting various comic marts at Westminster and Camden town halls. Here were dozens of dealers from all over the UK who gathered to sell back issues from huge long boxes perched on wooden trestle tables. Many comic creators attended these events, like Eddie Campbell, Ed Hilyer and Woodrow Phoenix. It was at one of these events that Alan Moore was introduced to Dave Gibbons. These marts also saw the entrepreneurial Paul Gravett setting up *Fast Fiction*, a stall where small press creators could sell their self-published comics for a small percentage. Paul moved on to publish *Escape* magazine so by the time I'd discovered these monthly comic fairs/social gatherings Ed Pinsent was running the stand and had set up a small photocopied anthology of the same name, showcasing the best talents around. This was all very inspirational to timid me, despite never really engaging with anyone at this stage.

After a year of misery I finally couldn't stand it any more and fled the tedious job at Austin Reed's in Windsor and the crappy bedsit in Eton and moved to my parent's place in Cranbrook. It was a leap of faith, straight into the fire. It was a tiny, two-bedroom cottage on a main road and next to a pub. Here I was, trapped in deepest Kent with no money, no friends, no job and no prospects. I was growing increasingly morose. I half-heartedly started writing several comic book concepts. Again, I was inspired by my dad, who in 1977 had a short Stephen King-esque story called *Jerome*, published in *Prima* women's magazine. I remember being incredibly impressed by this. My dad, a published author! Several years later he wrote to DC Comics inquiring about work there. He received a letter back from editor Archie Goodwin. The letterhead had, on the front, the DC bullet in green at the top, and on the back it had all DC's key superheroes standing on each other's shoulders, with Superman at the top with his arms wide open. When held up against the light the two images merged to show DC's roster of stars supporting the logo. The contents of the letter were just as encouraging. "While we don't have any openings as yet," Archie explained, "I would be interested to see anything if you'd like to try out for *Firestorm*." Firestorm was a C-List DC superhero who had his own title and had gone through three or four complete character revamps in so many years. They never quite knew what to do with him, and I guess Dad didn't either, as, to my dismay, he never followed this up.

I half-heartedly started writing several comic book treatments, literally bashed out on my beautiful beast of an Underwood No. 5 typewriter (the non-electric sort). But in those days before the Internet I lacked guidance, feedback or any connectivity with fellow writers and comic fans. I even naively tried writing drunk on whiskey, in some misguided belief that I might start channelling Hemingway's genius. I ended up just getting smashed, unable to type a coherent sentence, and failing to blow my brains out with a shotgun.

I had no money to get to London, or anywhere, and could barely afford to eat little but carbs, salts and sugars. My diabolically poor culinary skills and lack of funds meant I was living on white rice and soya sauce, and varying my diet with pasta and ketchup.

Somehow I scraped enough money together to make it back up to London for 1987's UKCAC, which had moved to a bigger venue at Logan Hall, Institute of Education on Bedford Way. Knowing what to expect this time, I'd booked a box room in the halls of residence for the Saturday night, and I was somewhat bolder. I'd learnt that artists would do sketches for you if you asked nicely, or bought them a pint, so armed with a little ring-bound black A6 notebook I started talking to anyone with a name badge.

I managed to get sketches from Jim McCarthy (Brendan's brother), a young-and-up-and-coming Steve Pugh, Cam Kennedy, and Mick McMahon.

I remember the first time I saw a very drunk Glenn Fabry. He was staggering around in the events hall and on the stage, having spent Saturday afternoon propping up the convention bar, followed by a coterie of fawning fanboys. At the time Glenn was justifiably receiving huge acclaim for his incredible artwork on *Slaine* in *2000 AD*. Barely able to stand, Glenn obviously needed help, however, it seemed to me that these "fans" were just taking the piss, revelling in Glenn's drunken antics and laughing *at* him, rather than *with* him. The next day I saw one of the said fanboys wearing Glenn's guest badge with some smug arrogance, trying to pass himself off as the great man. I burned with rage at the twat.

There were 21 US guests over that year including Karen Berger (again); graphic novel pioneer and creator of *The Spirit*, Will Eisner; Art Spiegelman; Walt Simonson—who'd just completed a successful run on *Thor*; DC Comics' Publisher Jenette Khan; and DC's VP and Executive Editor, Dick Giordano. 1987 seemed to be a landmark year for creators. Future *Punisher* artist Laurence Campbell attended as an aspiring artist and Duncan (*Hellboy*) Fegredo, Simon (*2000 AD*)

Coleby, and Kev F (*Beano*, *Oink*, *Viz*) Sutherland all got their first professional work at, or shortly before, UKCAC '87.

It was also the last comic convention Alan Moore ever attended. I remember there was a vast queue for his signing which went out the doors and up one side of a tall staircase. Alan was at the pinnacle of his popularity. *Watchmen* had just finished and fans couldn't get enough of him. Limited to signing one item per person, I recall approaching the "Great Yeti of a man" nervously to get my copy of the collected *Swamp Thing* Vol 1 signed. I was lucky to get anything signed as the queue was vast and his time was limited, but he was a real gent (and always has been in all subsequent meetings, bar one). However, later, so the apocryphal tale goes, whilst visiting the toilet he was accosted by a fan, or fans (accounts vary). Outraged at not even having the breathing space to be able to relieve himself, Moore swore he wouldn't attend another UK or US comic convention. A promise he kept for a quarter of a century, until he decided to play N.I.C.E. (the Northampton International Comic Expo) in 2012.

Returning from London I was filled with hope and optimism about comics' future and my role in it. Which was immediately crushed by the reality of my situation when I reached home. I was stuck in the back of beyond with no experience, no qualifications and no references worth speaking of. This was all too depressing. I decided from that point on that I was going to make this happen, I was determined to work in comics. I just wasn't quite sure doing what. My art wasn't up to scratch. I didn't feel confident enough writing. What other job could I do? And how would I even get this mythical, non-existent job? All I knew was that I wanted to be around comic creators.

"Get to know everybody" I thought. "How do I do that?" Then I had an inspiration, "Get a job in a comic shop." So, I stopped talking to myself, sat down at my (t)rusty typewriter and started hammering out letters to every comic shop in London.

CHAPTER TWO
"THANKS A LOT! BUY!"

"Thenceforth, I entered a jasmine-scented dream of the future."

—Rogan Gosh, Peter Milligan & Brendan McCarthy

Almost three months later, having sent out my hand-typed CV and a cover letter to every comic shop I could find in the London metropolitan area, asking for a job, I'd heard back from exactly none. Disheartened was an understatement. My last, best hope at working in comics lay broken and bloodied, shipwrecked on the shores of indifference. That was it, then. I had to abandon my dream of working in comics and resign myself to a menial job in retail. Apparently my destiny was to spend the rest of my days measuring rude, corpulent businessmen for suits.

But my love for the medium remained undiminished, despite comics seemingly ignoring me. That year Superman celebrated his 50th birthday and the newspapers were awash with articles. Even such literary luminaries as A.N. Wilson wrote about the "flying boy scout" in the *Daily Mail*. The *Radio Times* (4-10 June 1988) ran a Dave Gibbons cover and three-page strip, illustrating the radio play, *The Trial of Superman*, broadcast that week in celebration. The cover had Superman flying towards the reader whilst bursting out of a birthday cake, holding aloft a vintage BBC microphone. In my sad, fanboy obsessive way I cut these out (and many other comic-related magazine and newspaper articles) and kept them in a scrapbook that also doubled-up as my analogue checklist/comics wants journal.

Then, one day, a small envelope with a tiny A5 note in it popped through my letterbox. In the top right hand corner it had a picture of The Joker dealing out cards, drawn by Marshall Rogers. Underneath were the words "Comic Showcase".

It was from the owner, Paul Hudson, who casually thanked me for my interest and if I was ever in the area, I should pop in for a chat.

I'd never even heard of "London's Largest Comic Shop", despite it existing since 1980, much less visited it on my many comic-buying sorties to the West End. But that didn't matter. It was the only reply I'd got—or would ever get. I had to seize the opportunity. As soon as I could I rang the shop and arranged an interview.

Comic Showcase was based at the end of Neal Street (No. 76) on the fringes of trendy Covent Garden. Unbeknownst to me at the time, this was the shop's third location, having moved there from round the corner at 15 Catherine Street on the 30th of August, 1986. And before that, it had a tiny shop in Monmouth Street. But Showcase's latest venue was far more salubrious. Neal Street was peppered with hip clothes and shoe shops, bijou delis, and over-priced designer gift shops, and Showcase felt slightly incongruous in this setting. A massive window dominated the shop's front, displaying all sorts of comics and comic-related ephemera, from Captain America T-shirts to *Far Side* mugs and *Calvin and Hobbes* collections. The exterior was painted black with a double door, to the right of the window, which only ever had one of the doors open, except on special occasions, or very hot weather. Above the window swung a pub-like sign, which simply read: COMIC SHOWCASE in large red caps with a yellow drop shadow in a sans serif font on a black background.

Inside, the shop resembled a long, wide corridor. As you entered, a giant red and white chequered rocket spinner from Tintin's *Destination Moon* greeted you with all of Herge's adventures racked inside. To the right of that were shelves of newspaper cartoon reprints from *Bloom County*, *Doonesbury* and the like. The till was to your left, placed on a large white desk, which was crammed with the latest trade paperback collections, the Marvel Vault reprint series, and other books. The floor was a murky brown, hard-wearing carpet and down one long wall ran 100 feet of shelving where the latest comics sat, face out. Through the middle of the shop ran a large shelving unit with books and magazines on each side, with a gap in the middle to allow "easy" access. Following this all the way to the back of the shop you'd come to the back issue section where all the previous month's, and the months' before that, comics would be kept. On the back walls were dark brown cork tiles, with all the more expensive comics for the rich connoisseurs, pinned up, on display, but out of reach. Silver Age and Golden Age comics, classic EC titles and rarities of all kinds were on display to tempt those who had the cash, and taunt those who hadn't. On the back wall was a large ceramic Joker's mask. It was the lower part of a face, a white nose with ruby lips parted in a rictus grin revealing snowdrop teeth. Batman's nemesis, The Joker, was the shop's theme and "mascot" and various versions of the character appeared on bags and stationery over the years. The shop took its name, and mascot, from DC Comics. All the positive signs were there. The runes had been cast.

Paul greeted me and we went downstairs to his chaotic basement office piled with long boxes full of comics, stacks of paperwork all over the desk and mounds of T-shirts everywhere. Like many comic shops of that era, it smelled of damp and must. Showcase was— as regular customer Anthony Antoniou said on his *Stray Bullets* website—"Slightly crowded, messy, dusty, shambolic and utterly magical." But none of that deterred my attempts at impressing Paul with my comics knowledge (which was woefully scant) and sheer enthusiasm for the medium (which was practically evangelical). I must have made an impact with my impassioned plea to work in his shop because while he said he had no jobs going at that point, he'd let me know if any arose. I left London and headed back to

Cranbrook with mixed emotions. True, I didn't get a job, but I was on a promise. One that came through a few months later in 1988 when Paul, good to his word, rang up and said there was a position free if I wanted it. I was elated.

I spent the next year facing the gruelling commute from Cranbrook to Covent Garden. This would involve a 5-mile bus ride to Staplehurst train station, changing at Tonbridge, another train to Charing Cross and then a 10-minute walk to the shop. It took two hours each way, which meant leaving at 8am and getting home at 8:30-9pm at the earliest.

My fellow workmates were a great bunch of guys. There was "Rube", "Stick", "John Boy/J.B.", "Larry", and the boss, Paul "Fuddy" Hudson. Rube was the master of the till, serving everyone who came in. Short, hirsute, swarthy and wearing glasses, he was the eldest and longest serving member of the gang. His comics knowledge was unparalleled, although he had an unfortunate tendency to spray spittle on you when overly enthused on a topic.

Stick looked like a skinhead thug in his skin-tight jeans, shaved, blonde hair, Doctor Martin boots, and black leather biker jacket. To the layman he looked like a vicious thug, but in reality he was the softest spoken, most gentle bloke I'd ever met. He was a poet at heart, and his exterior acted like a Batesian mimic—a hoverfly pretending to be a wasp.

J.B. was a second-generation Kilburn Irish "fella". Stocky with a blonde flat top, he had a sharp wit and a cheeky demeanour.

Larry, so called for his wild, curly, unkempt hairstyle—Larry the Lamb—was the spitting image of a young Bob Dylan. A Hackney lad, he was lanky, with an undernourished appearance, like Stick. He was also a very talented artist, producing his own small-press comics.

Plus, there was an assortment of regulars who occasional worked part-time to pay for their monthly addictions, including handsome Asian chap, "Cheeky".

As the new boy, I was shoved right at the back of the shop where I bagged endless comics. I should explain, for the neophyte comics reader—comic shops would seal every single comic in a clear protective plastic bag which had a flap that was folded over and attached with one or two strips of sellotape (depending on your preferred style) on the back. They would leave a few reading copies out, but everything else was sealed up in a giant comic condom. With anything from 10 to 200 copies of 20-30 titles arriving every week it was the staff's job to make sure all these—potentially, 6,000 comics—were snugly packed, price stickered and put out on the shelves. There are three ways of protecting comics:

1) A simple bag.
2) For more expensive comics—£2.50 and above—you'd add a backing board—a piece of acid-free white card stiffener to prevent the spine being cracked or creased.
3) The deluxe Mylar sleeve. This plastic sleeve was open at the top but made of hard stiff clear plastic which helped keep UV rays from harming the comic inside. For additional safety a backing board would also be added for the top of the range comics.

Apart from the endless bagging, my other duty was to take down the Silver Age (comics published roughly between 1956 and 1970) and Golden Age comics (1938-1950), from the walls behind me, for prospective buyers to examine their condition. To a collector, the difference between a couple of creases on a spine or a small tear on a back cover could take the grade from NM (Near Mint) down to Very Fine (VF)—a difference that could be a couple of hundred quid.

Invariably, displaying these comics meant that I was talking to the richest customers and collectors. Chaps like Frank Mottler, "Chuck", Duncan McAlpine and BBC DJ and presenter Paul Gambaccini would frequently pop by to check out the latest acquisitions Fuddy had made either on buying trips to the States—picking up stock from New York comic dealer Gary Dolgoff—or by people selling their deceased relatives' collections to the shop. I enjoyed chatting to these comics connoisseurs and they expanded my knowledge enormously. But too lengthy a conversation would often receive an admonishment from Paul, "Oi, Pilch! Stop yakking and get bagging!"

Shortly after I'd started, Paul had agreed to take part in a charity fundraising event where various celebrities would work in their favourite shop for the day. "Alternative rock musician" Billy Bragg and TV presenter Jonathan Ross were to spend Saturday working behind the till at Showcase. "It'll make a nice change", said Wossy in a magazine article, "I'll be doing an honest day's work for a change and not just ligging around." Unfortunately, the same article reported that Comic Showcase was a "joke shop"! Bragg and Ross were regulars at Showcase and—as true comics aficionados—always knew exactly what they were talking about. Billy's first album (*Life's a Riot with Spy Vs Spy*) was named after a *MAD* magazine strip, and as early as 1988 Jonathan was writing newspaper articles like "Are you adult enough for comics?", abusing his celebrity to champion the new wave of mature titles: "Do yourself a big favour. Go and buy one, PLEASE!"

On the Saturday they worked it was a hot summer's day and we were absolutely mobbed. Billy worked in the morning and then popped next door to do an impromptu duet with Hank Wangford, while Jonathan took the afternoon shift. The shop was crammed with teenage girls and camera crews trying to film for that night's news. Jonathan was suited and booted as per usual, with his immaculately conceived hair, and signing posters for his *Incredibly Strange Picture Show* TV series. The deal was that in order to get an autograph you had to buy something, as 50% of the takings went to the charity. They managed to raise a lot of money for AIDS charities, while I spent most of the day quietly bagging at the back, chatting to the odd bemused regular.

Wossy was such a regular face in the shop I got to know him very well, to the point where we could ring up his production company and secure backstage passes whenever they were recording his TV show, *The Last Resort*, down at the ITV studios on the South Bank. One afternoon, after a particularly awkward live TV interview with the lead singer of The Fall, the previous night, the dapper presenter stormed around the shop and asked me, "Mark E. Smith. Genius or cunt?" Slightly taken aback by the language I won't tell you my reply, but suffice to say, the customer is always right.

It was also during this time that the bizarre, but mercifully brief, phenomenon of Bros. occurred. Bros. were a pop trio made up of Luke and Matt Goss and "the other one" (bassist Craig Logan) who got to number 2 of the UK charts with *When Will I be Famous?* Their management office was at the other end of Neal Street, next to Carluccio's original restaurant—where Jamie Oliver first worked—and their fans, the self-styled "Brosettes", got wind of this and consequently made the street their official hangout point. Occasionally, we'd get girls wandering into the shop dressed in the complete Brosette uniform: blue denim jeans and jacket, with a red neckerchief tied about their person and a couple of Grolsch beer bottle tops on their shoes. Where they sourced these latter items I don't know, as they were all well under drinking age. They would mooch about Showcase, unimpressed, and then leave. This was a comic shop for comics people, there was nothing for them here.

Sporadically Bros. would make an appearance and run down the street with the fans screaming and chasing after them. It was a bit like Pamplona, except with overly hormonal teenage girls instead of bulls.

Years later, Luke Goss managed to redeem his street cred somewhat, by becoming a competent actor, playing villains in two Guillermo del Toro comic book movies, *Blade II* (2002) and *Hellboy II: The Golden Army* (2008). However, he later blew it in an interview, "I'm becoming a geek bit by bit. If you don't know what you're talking about with these comic book fans, you're in trouble." Which instantly put him right back down to Freddie Starr's hipster rating.

I met more celebrities working at Showcase than at any other time before or since. Regular customers included musicians Dave Vanian (lead singer of The Damned), Marco Pirroni from Adam and the Ants, S'Express' Mark Moore, jazz musician Courtney Pine, Glenn Gregory and Martyn Ware of Heaven 17, comedians Vic Reeves and Bob Mortimer, Lenny Henry, and authors Christopher Fowler and Terry Jones. Fashion designer, and early rave organiser, Nick Coleman had a shop just down the road and would also hang out in Showcase when things were quiet.

One high point, for me, was a short, heavily bearded man with a baseball cap pulled down over his eyes. As he came up to the till I thought I recognised him. He spoke with an American accent and it fell into place. It was one of my comedy heroes, Robin Williams. He was obviously trying to avoid being recognised, so discretion took over and we chatted about the vast stack of graphic novels he was buying, including the by-now-obligatory *Watchmen*. At the time Terry Gilliam was rumoured to be directing the film adaptation, and it was known that Robin was interested in starring. Paying with a big wad of cash, he left knowing that, I knew that he knew, that I knew who he was, but I hadn't let on.

Six months later a very different Williams returned, clean-shaven and ebullient, with ex-*Monty Python* member Eric Idle in tow. I asked Williams if he enjoyed the books and he was quite chatty. When he started to get into a muddle with the different currencies he was carrying, Idle joined him in an improvised comedy skit. The experience of having two of my comedy heroes performing a very funny personal routine for me was so mind-blowing that, to this day, I can't recall the details. And that has to be possibly one of the worst anecdotes you'll ever have the misfortune to read. Unless you picked up Geri Halliwell's autobiography.

But, for me, the best thing about Showcase was meeting the *really* famous people; the comic creators I'd grown up reading. Most of them were *2000 AD* and *Warrior* luminaries like Brian Bolland, Dave Gibbons, Mick McMahon, David Lloyd and John Bolton—and they were all regulars at the shop. Thursday was "new comics day" when we'd get that week's deliveries in, and this collection of comic superstars arrived to pick up the latest titles, hang out and chat. Best of all, I became friends with my two artistic childhood heroes, Steve Dillon and Garry Leach. They say, "never meet your heroes, you'll only be disappointed," but neither has let me down yet. A more booze-soaked pair of reprobates I have yet to meet. Actually, that's not true. But we'll get to the rest later.

Garry "Letch" Leach and fellow cohort Dave "Spud" Elliott had formed Atomeka Press and were putting together their excellent anthology, *A1*, that they launched in 1989. They used Showcase as a "Post/Art and Restroom Service" hanging out in the shop and showing us the original artwork as it came in from talents such as

Barry Windsor Smith, Eddie Campbell, Glenn Fabry, Peter Milligan, Brendan McCarthy and Ted McKeever.

The young journalist from the *Today* newspaper, Neil Gaiman, had moved on considerably, and his star was in the ascendant—having written the *Violent Cases* graphic novel and the DC Comics *Black Orchid* miniseries with Dave McKean (which "guest-starred" Garry, Dave and Fleetway's then-PR guru, Igor Goldkind as the villain). Gaiman was now going great guns with *The Sandman*. Once a month Neil would pop in the shop to pick up the latest titles and very kindly leave me with the photocopies of the pencils for the forthcoming issues—of what would become one of his seminal works—while he browsed the shelves or caught up with fellow pros. Unfortunately, he would invariably arrive late on a Thursday afternoon, our most manic period of the week, and I hadn't the heart to tell him I was far too busy on the till to read them. So, more often than not, I just returned *The Sandman* photocopies unread with a non-committal, "Looks great! Looking forward to it coming out!" (Sorry, Neil!) However, I was, and still am, a big fan of his work. There was a slightly disingenuous ongoing joke in the shop about leaving any of his books and comics near him as he would sign anything with impunity. But I'll confess, I never saw him signing anything he wasn't asked to, so I suspect this is apocryphal. Yet this myth still perpetuates to this day.

Thursdays in Showcase were always crazy. The Titan Distribution van, driven by "Camp Bob", would usually pull up around midday and everyone would rush out to unload the boxes as quickly as possible, as it blocked the road. Then, all the comics had to be counted off against the delivery note, bagged and put on the shelves while the passionate—sorry, make that rabid—fans hovered around waiting to grab the first copies. This was at the height of the speculator market, when people were buying 10-20 copies of new titles in the vain hope that they would massively appreciate in value. The hardcore "mint boys" would literally lurk over us and try and take the best condition ones straight out of the box before we'd even had a chance to count them, and we had to tell them to back off in no uncertain terms. It was when the majority of the regulars would come in and we'd be frantically bagging and restocking the shelves all day. It was also the day when, after we shut the shop, we'd pop down along Neal Street to Frank's (actually run by Salvatore) for a quick bite to eat. Then we'd decamp with a few of the regulars to The Two Brewers pub in Seven Dials for several pints and a long discussion about sequential art.

Two favourites with the Showcase staff were *Reid Fleming* by David Boswell and Dave Sim's controversial *Cerebus*—both created by Canadians. Fleming was "The World's Toughest Milkman", a no-nonsense, obnoxious, box-shaped-nosed pugilist who was just as likely to piss on your flowers as he was deliver cow juice to your door. It was surreal, absurdist and we loved it. *Cerebus* on the other hand, had its surreal moments, but was much more thought-provoking. It started out as a slightly crap *Conan* parody featuring Cerebus the Aardvark, but soon developed into a political satire featuring a whole host of recognisable pastiches, from Groucho Marx and Mick Jagger to various superheroes, such as Wolverine and Moon Knight. The complexity and sheer scale of the project (300 issues, all written and drawn by Sim and his assistant Gerhard) was impressive. At the time it was the most intelligent comic on the shelves, but unfortunately Sim's increasingly misogynistic views and erratic stances on religion meant the series ultimately ended after 27 years with a whimper rather than a bang.

By now, I was also whimpering, as the daily commute from Kent was really killing me. If I went out for a drink after work, which I invariably did on a Thursday night, I would inevitably miss the last bus from Staplehurst train station back to Cranbrook, and have to face a five-mile walk home. Most times I was lucky enough to thumb a lift, but I'd get in at 1am and be up at 7am ready to head back into London. This couldn't continue. Regardless of the physical exhaustion, it was costing me a fortune in fares. Money I could've been spending on comics.

One of the many fortunate things about working in Showcase was meeting a huge network of Comic Showcase/Two Brewers regulars. I soon made friends with Martin Hand, Fiona Jerome, Nigel Fletcher, Gerard Kingdon, Tim and Pippa Bateman, Howard Stangroom, Guy Lawley and numerous others. This clique welcomed me with open arms and it was through them I met James Wallis. James had a house in Edmonton and was looking for someone to rent a room. Fortunately, I fitted the bill (i.e. not insane, a comic fan, and with enough rent money) and so moved in. This was the start of my decade-long love affair with London.

Many of those friends, including James, were involved in the Amateur Press Association (APA) scene. These were anthology based fanzines created by members, collated, photocopied and circulated to all the contributors, who paid a small dividend or "sub" to cover printing and postage. Essentially, they were analogue social networking—a paper-based Facebook. There were hundreds of these, each one acting as a creative forum for niche interest groups, such as *APA-247*, which dealt specifically with DC Comics' Legion of Super Heroes. I joined *BAPA* (British Amateur Press Association) and started contributing some woefully inept pieces (a particularly bad "rap" by a pig springs to mind for the "Bacon" issue). Each issue had a theme chosen by a different member and it taught me how to deliver work to order, and on time, even if it wasn't very good.

Meanwhile, at work, Showcase was one of the few shops to sell original comic art, and thus it became a hub for all the top talent in the UK. We saw nearly all the key art in comics history pass through the shop. Paul dealt with US art dealer Scott Dunbier (at time of writing, special projects editor at IDW), who had access to practically every artist Stateside. Numerous *Dark Knight Returns* pages by Frank Miller and Klaus Janson were sold at Showcase (prices now reach $250,000 per page). Plus, we had exclusive deals with all of Kevin O'Neill's *Marshall Law* artwork, all of David Lloyd's *V for Vendetta* art and all the pages from *Watchmen* by Dave Gibbons (with a few notable exclusions). I bought a page of *Watchmen* art. I spent a lot of money on artwork, comics and related ephemera in the shop. A lot of money. Far too much money. In fact, so much money, that I was in hock to Hudson for hundreds of pounds. Paul, in his clever, capitalistic way, decided to exploit my comic book addiction by opening the shop on Sundays and allowing me to work off my credit. I felt like a miner trapped in debt bondage. For every £30 I worked off my tab, I then added another £40 in comics fixes. It got to the point that management tried to get me to just borrow books to read, rather than buying them, as it looked as if I was going to be eternally indebted. "I owed my soul to the company store."

By now my comic book addiction/affliction had reached its zenith. For some bizarre reason I'd set myself the challenge of collecting every single appearance of DC Comics' horror character, Swamp Thing (created by Len Wein and Berni Wrightson) and Mark Evanier and Sergio Aragonés' Conan parody, Groo the Wanderer. Why I picked those two characters I still don't know, maybe just because I enjoyed them. And when I said "every single appearance" I didn't just mean every comic, I meant even the slightest cameo in the back of a panel, somewhere drawn into a completely irrelevant panel of an unrelated comic by some unconnected artist. Every. Single. Appearance. I was temporarily insane at this point.

With comic collecting the thrill is in the chase, the hunt. The actual acquisition is less important—it's the journey, not the destination. Collecting comics has often been equated to trainspotting, and certainly there's something of the Asperger's Syndrome common in both hobbies—the obsessive collecting and sorting of an object, date, number or thing. I was in a privileged position working in the shop, as many comics passed through there from various collections we sold and so I could cherry-pick the key issues I was looking for.

Then, after several years, I had my epiphany. I'd actually achieved my goal. I'd successfully managed to get *every single* appearance of Swamp Thing and Groo that had ever been drawn in a professional comic book. Every guest appearance, background sketch or visual nod. *Everything!* Barring any future publications, which I could pick up easily, there was nowhere to go after that. I'd finally reached the summit and the view was suddenly clear to me. Sure, I could have moved on to another character, making it harder and more expensive for myself (collecting every single appearance of Batman, for example) but I'd had my Damascene conversion. I'd seen the futility of it all. From that point on I stopped collecting comics for the sake of completionism and just bought them to read and enjoy. The relief and weight off my shoulders was palpable. I was no longer a slave to the four-colour funnies, rather I was the master of my purchases. Sadly, my comics reading list was still vast and voracious, but at least I was not *obliged* to actually buy *everything*.

Unfortunately, for my wallet, 1988 was the year I discovered manga and anime. Thanks to the late Toren Smith's English translations of series like Kazuya Kudo and Naoki Urasawa's *Pineapple Army*, Yoshihisa Tagami's *Grey* and *Nausicaä of the Valley of the*

Wind by Hayao Miyazaki. Then Katsuhiro Otomo's *Akira* exploded everywhere. It was, as artist Frank Quitely said, "A gateway drug" into manga. A whole new world of bizarre pop culture opened out in front of me, full of vivid graphics, screaming voices, speedlines and incomprehensible plots. I was hooked. There were several Showcase regulars who shared my passion and we swapped creaky, eighth-generation copy VHS tapes of anime shows. They weren't dubbed or subtitled, but we didn't care. In the days before the Internet this was the only way of "file-sharing". Our obsession for this alien art form went to the extremes of making weekly visits to the Japan Centre near St. Paul's Cathedral in a lunch break, to pick up the latest imports. Again, none of this was translated, but the graphics, typography and design were so exciting, fresh and original, we didn't care that we couldn't actually read the damn things!

1988's UKCAC took place on 24-25 September. While in the convention bar on Saturday afternoon, I got chatting to a gang of former art students from the South Coast called Jamie Hewlett, Alan Martin, and Philip Bond, who were up for the weekend. As we were chatting they explained they had work in a new magazine coming out called *Deadline*. Just as we were talking the writers/artists/editors/founders of *Deadline*, Brett Ewins and Steve Dillon (who I knew from the shop), appeared with a big stack of the first issue, literally hot off the press. On the front was a cartoon girl shaving her head. It was Tank Girl, drawn by Jamie, and she was to become a global phenomenon and a cultural icon for a generation.

I instantly got on with the gang from Worthing, These talented mavericks were looking to shake things up and Mr Ewins gave them the platform to do it in the shape of *Deadline*, while the genial Tom Astor, a direct descendant of the famous Astor publishing family, funded the whole thing.

1988 also saw Glyn Dillon joining their ranks. Glyn was Steve's younger brother, and was a gorgeous looking chap. He was reminiscent of a younger, better-looking version of Alex James from Blur. He was, by his own admission, "Young, eager and a bit precocious…" as were all of the Worthing crowd. And rightly so, as they were all destined for greatness.

Apart from the bar and the costume parade, the other main highlight of the convention was the charity auction of all the artwork from the booklet. It was a chance for many to get an original work of art (in every sense) by their favourite comics artist at fairly reasonable prices and help other people out at the same time. However, UKCAC '88 saw a showdown that is still talked about to this day. That year's booklet had a painting by Dave McKean, of the Joker looking particularly menacing, with some playing cards revealing a hand of two aces and three deuces, and the scratchy title: "Hope it's a full house, guys!" Everyone was eagerly anticipating his and Grant Morrison's forthcoming *Arkham Asylum: A Serious House on Serious Earth* and everybody knew that Paul Hudson was a massive Joker fan, as the character was the symbol of Comic Showcase.

Normally, artwork would go for anything between £50-£150 depending on the artist and the subject matter. The auditorium was packed. There was a buzz going around "How much do you think it'll go for?" "Who's going to bid for it?" Hass, one of the show's organisers (and a Showcase regular), saved the Joker painting till last. He knew what he was doing.

Word had got around that Paul wanted the painting to hang in the shop. But also that Mike Lake, who owned rival shop Forbidden Planet, was interested. However, many suspected this counter interest was there merely to undermine Paul's bidding.

Mike wasn't present at the auction but had sent Jon Harrison (or Dick Jude – accounts differ) to secure the artwork "At *any* cost".

Paul and the rest of the Showcase crowd sat at the middle left-hand side of Logan Hall. He had a big wad of cash on him from the day's takings.

Hass started the proceedings with a shock.

"I'm going to start the bidding at £150."

A murmur rippled through the audience, "£150! That's a bit steep!" It was a gamble that sorted the wheat from the chaff. With the boys shut out, the men started bidding:

"£500!" Cried out an over-enthusiastic audience member.

"£600" shouted Paul.

"£750" Jon Harrison sparked up.

"£800" Said Paul.

The first bidder dropped out, the stakes already getting too high.

"£950"

Heads swivelled back and forth between the two bidders. It was a tense Wimbledon volley, the crowd waiting to see who blinked first.

"£1,100" Paul snapped the bid back across the net.

This went on for minutes, the audience getting more and more excited. Records were being smashed right before their eyes. Until the bidding reached:

"£1,500?"

"£1,500"

I looked at Paul. He was starting to fidget.

"£1,600" came the reply from across the hall.

"£1,700" Responded Paul, smiling nervously.

"£1,800?" Asked Hass.

Jon nodded.

"£1,900" Paul found himself saying.

"£2,000" Things were slowing down.

"£2,100?"

And then the bombshell, "No" said Paul, and turned to us and said, quietly, "I don't need it *that* bad."

Later, Paul said that he wasn't really bothered either way, but when he saw that Mike Lake was interested, he thought he'd try and push the price up as high as he could, as he knew Lake didn't really want the piece and was just out to scupper him. Always the joker, Paul had the last laugh. However, many suspect this was bravado, and that he was actually spitting feathers. I think, to this day, it still remains one of the most expensive pieces of artwork at any of the British comic convention auctions. That year the auction raised over £8,000 for Imperial Cancer Research Fund, Help the Aged and other charities, a quarter of it from that one, single painting. After, Mike apologised to Paul for forcing the price up and offered to sell the painting to him for £2,000. But it was too late, it had been tainted by then.

Back at Comic Showcase, I eventually progressed from the back of the shop to the middle bagging area, where all regulars picked up their standing orders, posters were handed over to customers, and the majority of creators hung out. I took on looking after the small press section, where enterprising creators brought their self-published titles in for us to sell on a "Sale Or Return" (SOR) basis. Here, I dealt with Ed Pinsent's Fast Fiction line. I actively encouraged and nurtured many up-and-coming talents and their publications, including: Andi Watson's *Samurai Jam*; Nabiel Kahan's *Exit*; Gary and Warren Pleece's *Velocity*; Sean Longcroft and Rob Davis' *Slang*, "an LSD-drenched journey through mundane suburbia"; Bob Lynch's range of *Sav Sadness* titles; *Arnie* by Simon Gane; Aidan Potts' *Inkling*; and Peter Pavement's excellent Slab-O-Concrete list of titles. While a few eventually left the industry disenchanted, the majority went on to be highly successful comics professionals.

I was inspired by all this creativity to actually get off my arse and self-publish my own egotistical rantings in *Tim True Stories*, a "slice-of-life" pamphlet based on my limited world experiences and inspired by the autobiographical work of Robert Crumb and Harvey Pekar. However, my woeful lack of drawing skill and lettering abilities meant these shambolic, not-very-good, strips were few and far between. I was also very slow at drawing. I realised that if I was going to produce anything, I was going to have to create an anthology and pad it with far more talented people than I. Fortunately there was no lack of those, and I managed to put together a rostrum of impressive creatives including: Brian Goldstein, Matt Meadows (older brother of *Tripwire* magazine publisher, Joel), Tony Gage, Ollie Sung, fellow co-worker Tony Lee, Andy Martin and my future flatmate, Pete (Count Libido) Weekes.

The following year (1989) was "The year of the Bat". Not only did Bruce Wayne turn 50, but Tim Burton's seminal film, *Batman*, was due that summer. Bat-mania had gripped the shop, and me, as I played Prince's film soundtrack incessantly. There hadn't been a big screen Batman movie in my lifetime (The last was Adam West and Burt Ward's hilarious outing in 1966). Paul H was over the moon with Jack Nicholson playing the Joker and we filled Showcase with every conceivable form of Bat-merchandise. The shop was crammed with bat tat: mugs, stickers, T-shirts, action figures, batmobiles, trading cards, posters, filofaxes, etc. etc. etc. All with Batman or the Joker emblazed upon it. And we sold it all. The country had caught Bat-fever as well.

In the days before the Internet, Showcase became a hub for meeting like-minded people and sharing and disseminating information and illegally received materials, such as film scripts that would be photocopied and passed on. I received a first draft of Sam Hamm's *Batman* script (dated 20 October 1986) this way—a 34th generation photocopy that is still hard to read today. This was gold dust back then, and many of the elements in this draft made it to the final screen version.

The whole shop—staff and regulars—went as an outing on the first night when the film finally opened. Burton didn't disappoint. Looking back, *Batman* feels a little faded around the edges and a tad hokey. But at the time it was dark, edgy and slightly scary—tapping in perfectly to the zeitgeist started by Frank Miller's *The Dark Knight Returns* (1986) and *Batman: Year One* (1987). Plus, it had the added bonus of raising the awareness of comics to the general public, and for a brief period the footfall in the shop increased.

I was eventually plonked on the till "because none of the rest of us wanted to do it and you were the new boy, so couldn't complain", recalled Stick. However, I was, as Stick put it, "the consummate fanboy. Whenever anyone famous came in you'd be straight over to say hi and find out what they were doing, while J.B. and I were hiding down the back pretending to be cool and uninterested". It was in Comic Showcase that I first met the artist John McCrea who was showing Stick his impressive portfolio. McCrea was a semi-regular visitor from Belfast who "had to get on a boat from Larne (a shit hole in Northern Ireland) to Stranraer (a shit hole in Scotland) and then travel 11 hours on a bus just to go to Comic Showcase". McCrea got one of his first breaks in comics in Showcase: "I got 'talent' spotted by Lionel Grace Whitman (publisher of *Heartbreak Hotel*), which led to *On Earth As It Is* in *Blaam!*, the short-lived, free, tabloid comic".

McCrea had also just started working on *Crisis*, painting *Troubled Souls*, which was written by a man who would become one of my oldest, best friends, Garth Ennis.

I finally, permanently, secured the prime location when both Stick and Rube "King of the Till" left for pastures new. I was made manager of the shop and Paul plonked me behind the cash register. Here I was running the shop when Paul was away at the other branches in Cambridge and Oxford. The power! Being on the till meant I could shill my *Tim True Stories* to every customer, as I shamelessly whored my wares out.

Unfortunately, sitting behind the till with my endlessly, annoyingly chipper demeanour meant I became an unofficial face of the shop. I'd even been labelled with my own prosaic catchphrase, which friends and regulars mercilessly repeated ad infinitum, "Thanks a lot, bye!" Publicity shy Paul always pushed me in front of the cameras when a Thames Television news crew wanted to talk to a "comics expert" about the latest hot comic news; such as the Christian fundamentalist who felt that *Teenage Mutant Ninja Turtles* was corrupting Britain's youth. "Nothing has been marketed so successfully in the history of mankind," he ranted, completely forgetting that Christianity had a good 2,000 years of marketing expertise over four terrapins with nunchakus.

Of course, my rambunctious ego didn't exactly dissuade me from being a glory hound either. I eventually managed to wrangle my way onto *Comic Cuts*, an appalling TV show about comics for kids. This was the early days of satellite TV, the "squarial" and BSB. Many small, independent channels and production companies popped up producing endless shows on miniscule budgets.

The producer was a customer and he asked if I'd like to get involved. I ended up appearing semi-regularly, being erratically introduced as everything from a "comic expert" to "young comic fan" and back again. I would head up to the tiny studio at Teddington Lock and sit on the small, sweaty set, where I was, not so much asked questions, as told statements, to which the only reply I could think of was the impotent "Indeed". When I was fed questions they were asinine ones that required equally asinine replies.

"So, Tim, what *exactly* is Comic Showcase?"
"It's a comic *shop!*"

Those four fateful words would hang around my neck like an albatross for years. Customers would come in and taunt me with it. Friends would create birthday cards with the slogan on it.

Mike, the presenter of *Comic Cuts*, was also the producer and was a tall, blonde, jolly chap in a sharp suit and tie. Unfortunately, he was also desperately condescending—as was the tone of the entire show. They had an aging cartoonist, Chris, who was a lovely guy with a scary beard and an eclectic taste in knitwear, who sounded permanently inebriated. Then there was me, the "Timbo the himbo", with my endlessly chirpy, Prozac-inspired, insipid grin, and poor choice of comic-related T-shirts. If there was ever a trio to scare kids off comics for life, we were it.

Realising the limits of my art and writing abilities on *Tim True Stories*, I decided to try my hand at colouring comics and took my friend Steve Whittaker's course at the London Cartoon Centre in Conlan Street, up from Notting Hill. Steve, or Witko as he was affectionately known (he was a massive Steve Ditko fan), was a fellow BAPA member and a huge talent. His skilful art and colouring was only matched by his complete lack of faith in his own abilities. It was tragic that someone with such talent could have so little belief in themselves. Consequently, nearly everything he produced ran late because he agonised about whether every line was just right. Everyone loved Steve, but his penchant for watching deadlines whoosh by meant he found it hard to get work. Editors felt they simply couldn't rely on him not to delay the book, much as they wanted to use him.

His comics knowledge eclipsed virtually everyone I knew and he was a giant, friendly bear of a man. With his greying, wildly unkempt, black, curly hair and long black coat, he would greet you with a huge tombstone smile, a wave, and a friendly booming "Hullo!"—and depart the same way with a "Cheery-bye!" Steve was part of the comics gang who'd taken me under their wing when I first moved to London, and he was a mentor to many, including Larry at Showcase, and artist Matt "D'Israeli" Brooker.

Steve was also one of the best colourists in the industry and will probably be best remembered for two main jobs, the first being his innovative work on *The New Adventures of Hitler* in *Crisis*. The strip was written by Grant Morrison and drawn by Steve Yeowell. Witko came along with Nick Abadzis and revolutionised colouring by creating blueline collages with images that complemented or juxtaposed Yeowell's line work, sometimes to the point of drowning out the original black and white art. The end result was electrifying and utterly unique. Steve's highest profile work was co-colouring the DC Comics version of *V for Vendetta*, alongside David Lloyd and Siobhan Dodds. While at Showcase, I bought a page of Steve's *V...* bluelines—the only completely silent page in the story— something I still treasure.

So, to be taught colouring by one of the best in the biz was a great honour, as was having his friendship. Steve clearly explained every step of the colouring process. In those days it was still done with colour separations. The colours would be a combination of cyan (C), magenta (M), yellow (Y) and black (K)[1]. Photocopies of the black and white artwork would then be coloured up using Dr. Martin's Dyes. These would then be marked up, based on a colour chart. This would include various percentages, usually 25%, 50% and 75%. For example, a nice mid-green would be marked up as "Y25C50K25", that is: 25% Yellow, 50% Cyan, 25% Black. These colour mark-ups would then be sent to the separators who would mark the plates up based on the guide—this was Nick Abadzis' (cartoonist and *Hugo Tate* and *Laika* graphic novelist) first job at Marvel UK. When each plate was eventually printed on top of each other, it would create a full colour image. This was an incredibly crude system that had been in place since the Thirties. But the recent introduction of "bluelines" was shaking things up. Blueline meant that fully painted artwork could be created on special photocopied artwork, which had the line work printed in non-repro blue. The colourist would paint over this and a black acetate would be laid over to reveal the original line art. Then the whole thing was shot by camera. This was a more expensive process, but as it got cheaper it allowed comics to make the leap from black and white line drawings coloured, to fully painted works of art. This technological leap helped make stars of artists like Simon Bisley, Dermot Power and Greg Staples in the pages of the glossier looking *2000 AD*.

I learnt everything I could from Steve, about the concepts of colour and its use in portraying mood, emotion, highlighting elements in a picture, pushing characters into the background and bringing them forward, tonal variations, etc. Rich, vast, incredible knowledge—which I did absolutely bugger all with. By the time I'd seriously thought about actually trying to get a colouring job,

---

[1] It was a K to stand for Key, which all the other colours had to align to, and not so it wouldn't get confused for a blue, rather than a black.

the entire industry had moved on to computers, and colour separation work was a defunct technology. It's all digital and Photoshop these days.

A few years later Steve, amazingly, asked me to help him out with the junior Saturday morning classes at the London Cartoon Centre, and I had a lot of fun teaching kids about pacing, page construction, lettering, basic anatomy and the like. Hopefully I atoned for the damage I'd done on *Comic Cuts*. Tragically, Steve collapsed from a massive stroke on 22 February 2008. In the words of Morrissey he was "The first of the gang to die". I miss him a lot.

As manager of the shop I managed to take certain liberties, such as using Showcase as a personal after hours clubhouse in the heart of the West End. I opened the shop up for friends to have a pre-pub toke in the basement and tried impressing girls by bringing them back after an evening of drinks. I was stunned when I went to a preview screening of *True Romance*, only to see the lead character, Clarence (Christian Slater), doing exactly the same thing on screen! He'd even, bizarrely, worked in the comic shop the same amount of time as me.

The other liberty I took was spending more "chat time" with the established and rising stars of comics. One of the loveliest was the artist Paul Johnson, whose work I'd first seen briefly in *pssst!* magazine, all those years ago. His fly-away, faintly reddish hair, glasses, goatee and perennial black leather jacket was topped off with a smile as ubiquitous as his jacket. In fact I seem to recall Paul being even more smiley than me. Perhaps that's why we hit it off.

He'd self-published his *Modern Eyes* magazine, "The zenith of mongoloid reasoning" in 1985, but got his big break illustrating James Robinson's graphic novel, *London's Dark*. It was published by

Paul Gravett and Peter Stanbury's Escape imprint, alongside Gaiman and McKean's *Violent Cases*.

I remember going round to Paul's flat in Borehamwood one hot summer's afternoon in 1990 to interview him for a magazine—I was failing to get a writing career off the ground by doing odd bits of comics "journalism" on the side. He asked if I would pose for him, as he worked from photographs. Flattered, and slightly wary as to whether it would involve me removing all my clothes, I obliged. The results appeared in the *Hellraiser/Nightbreed: Jihad* two-parter written by Dan Chichester. That was the start of a long "working" relationship and close friendship with Paul, posing for a whole range of comics, which spanned seven years.

Those sessions were always lots of fun and were mostly held at the basement flat in Paddington belonging to Paul's girlfriend, Ellie. She was a former teacher who'd jacked it in to become a comic book letterer for various publishers. It was like running away from home to join a firm of chartered accountants. With less pay and glamour. Paul's posing sessions usually happened in the evenings, and occasionally at weekends. Running for anything between 2-4 hours, they often involved copious alcoholic refreshments and holding brooms or toy guns, as if being attacked by some imaginary monster, or dangling off stepladders in awkward and uncomfortable positions, while Paul got the right shot. He was always an excellent director, talked us through the script, explaining the story and getting the best emotive reactions. We were generously remunerated with free beer all evening, a meal out after the session and a page of artwork. More than fair compensation.

I wasn't the only one who modeled for Paul, and in fact nearly everyone I knew back then posed at some point including Woodrow Phoenix (back when he was plain old Trevs), Ilya, Dick Hansom, the late Phil Gasgoine, Paul Hudson, my then-girlfriend Yasmin. You name it; we're all in there!

I used to joke that Paul and Ellie were my "surrogate parents", as they took me under their wing, and introduced me to another world of late night parties and recklessness. It was through them that I first met Senior DC Editor Art Young (not to be confused with the late 19th century cartoonist—if such a thing was possible. He wasn't dead for a start). Paul was working on a one-shot comic called *Mercy* that J. M. DeMatteis had written for Art's Touchmark comic company.

Art cut a distinctive figure. Standing around 6' 1" with foppish light brown hair and often dressed in horizontal striped T-shirts and beads. He had a youthful, boyish charm—despite being ten years older than me—and a quick flashing smile. Joel Meadows described him in *Tripwire* magazine as "...Shaggy from *Scooby-Doo*. Or perhaps one of the Brand New Heavies... He looked like a side-burned, cappuccino-supping bohemian from Hell". Art was also charming, quick-witted and gregarious to the max. I liked him instantly. Little did I know it, but he was to have a profound effect on my life.

One quiet Wednesday afternoon in Showcase Stuart Goddard, better known as "The King of the Wild Frontier", "The Dandy Highwayman" and "Prince Charming", popped into the shop and mooched around. The layout of Showcase meant that it was pretty easy to spot people when they came in and so all the staff had eyeballed him early on. It probably wasn't that surprising he was there, seeing as his ex-lead guitarist, Marco, was a semi-regular. Eventually he struck up a conversation with me on the till and it turned out that he was a big Tank Girl fan and was trying to get in touch with Jamie Hewlett. Now, I'm not in the habit of handing people's numbers out willy nilly, but I figured "Who wouldn't want Adam Ant to give them a call?", so, conveniently, I happened to have Jamie's telephone number on me and passed it on to Adam, and thought no more about it.

Around that time it felt like every weekend there were at least eight different comic-related parties to go to. If it wasn't a launch party down at the Acme Comic Shop on Coldharbour Lane in Brixton, it was a gallery opening for a *Deadline* art exhibition in a trendy hairdressers in Camden. Not to mention the endless house parties various creators were throwing.

Deadline was doing phenomenally well, and comics in general were being lauded as the new rock'n'roll. Unsurprising then, that *Deadline* held a huge birthday party at the deconsecrated church-cum-nightclub, The Limelight, in the heart of the West End. I got there way too early and found myself nursing a drink when this big bloke in a cowboy hat walked up to me and said in a thick Staffordshire accent, "This is a bit shite, innit?" I turned to him, staring at the long Zapata moustache and three growths on his face and realised it was Lemmy from Motorhead. I replied that it was a bit early. He then proceeded to bore the arse off me, trying to make small talk and failing miserably. I pretended to go to the toilet and lurked in another part of the club where I couldn't be seen. Eventually the party picked up and there were a string of live bands that had some association with the magazine, including CUD—whose bassist, William Potter, drew *Nommo* in *Deadline*. There was a painful Tank Girl look-a-like competition with somebody in a pathetic kangaroo costume, but overall, it was a top night out with free booze. And the free booze and partying kept on flowing.

Somehow, by 1991, I managed to wrangle myself onto the Small Press Panel at UKCAC alongside Meanwhile... shop owner Mike O'Donoghue, Dave (*Downside*) McNamara, my old Edmonton housemate—and unrecognised comics genius—Martin Hand,

Bob (*Sav Sadness*) Lynch, Aidan (*Inkling*) Potts, Larry Watson and Graham Johnstone. Theo Clarke moderated the panel, where I told the audience how I funded *Tim True Stories* "…Solely out of my own pocket. You just literally say 'Well, there's £25-£50' and just throw it away. You don't expect to see that coming back; and you produce the comic. If you get anything back, as I say, it's a plus, but you have to be prepared to start off with making a loss and waiting for at least two or three issues before you can start seeing money coming back in, and it does take a long time."

I don't think I ever made a profit on *TTS*, and it existed completely on the kindness of strangers. But I was passionate about advancing the medium, "There is so much more out there with the comic narrative you can do sensibly and intelligently, which the mainstream publishers aren't doing…We can eventually start a new genre. Superheroes take up 95% of the market. If we can change that into more realistic comics, more intelligent stuff then that's what we're trying to do, just make comics fans think a bit more."

My passion got the better of me and I started to rant, "Listen we're all sitting around saying 'We should do this, we should do that' When are we actually going to see some action? When are we actually going to get down together, everyone together, and start actually creating an organisation which is going to do this?"

Fortunately Martin's levity was on hand, "In the bar!"

"In the bar, afterwards." I agreed

"Don't forget it's Sunday, it's three o'clock closing-time," Martin said, sagely reminding us of the true priorities in life.

UKCAC '91 also saw Art Young over, promoting his new comics publishing company, which was to launch the following Spring.

Art's career path started out as Karen Berger's assistant at DC Comics working on *Doom Patrol, Animal Man, Wonder Woman*, the US-reworking of *V for Vendetta*, and numerous other titles. After a few years, he was growing restless and was lured over to the West Coast by Disney who wanted to set up a new line of adult-friendly—but not pornographic—comics. Tying in with their film studio, Touchstone, the comics line was named Touchmark, "Which still sounds more than faintly seedy, I feel," recalled Grant Morrison, "I still have the badges which read 'Touchmark - Deal With It!' and again, hint at some vague, damp, abusive encounter with the unsuspecting writer of the *X-Ultimates*." Art managed to lure many DC creators over with him to work on numerous creator-owned projects.

That UKCAC he was on a panel in the same hall two hours after our small press one, and giving away badges and flyers promoting the first three titles, *Enigma* by Peter Milligan and Duncan Fegredo, *Sebastian O* by Grant Morrison and Steve Yeowell, and *Mercy* by Marc DeMatteis and my friend, Paul Johnson. Very little actual work had been done on these titles and the art in it was all promotional, drawn specifically for the flyer. On it was a vast list of creators who Touchmark were going to allegedly publish, with the tagline "We can't help bragging about the company we keep." Art had learnt at DC that hyperbole worked and played it to the full. However, there were a lot of creators listed who never actually produced anything for Art in the end, such as John Wagner, Garry Leach, Richard Piers Rayner, George Pratt, Sam Kieth, John Bolton, Kent Williams, Kelly Jones and Simon Bisley.

The Touchmark flyer given out that year explained, "You won't find much mainstream superhero stuff here. Or sword-and-sorcery fantasy. If that's what you're looking for there's hundreds of titles on the shelves now that will give you just that. What you will find are some genres perhaps not usually associated with comics. Like drama. Or dramatic comedy. Real people in real situations set in the real world. Wow, what a concept, huh?" It was almost as if Art and I were reading from the same manifesto I'd been espousing two hours earlier.

"Is Touchmark for everybody?" The flyer continued, "Probably not. But we think there's enough of you out there that want something just a little bit different." This was to be the template for Vertigo.

Art flew back to California after UKCAC, to get ready for the big launch in five months' time. Here he was living it up in sunny L.A. with a great job, and his own publishing list. Then the metaphorical earthquake hit. Disney were suffering big time. In the days before Steve Jobs, John Lassiter and Pixar came to rescue them, the studio was floundering. Costs had to be saved. Cuts had to be made. And, as is so often the way, it was an unfortunate case of last in, first out. Touchmark was canned and Art had the rug pulled from under him. Suddenly, he had six projects and nowhere to publish them. Worse, he was out of a job. By an incredibly lucky twist of fate, Art's old DC boss, Karen, was looking to amalgamate a lot of her titles, such as *Swamp Thing*, *The Sandman*, *Animal Man*, *Hellblazer*, *Shade The Changing Man* and others into a new adult comics line.

He moved back to New York, while he co-devised the Vertigo strategy with Karen. Over the next six months he shared an apartment with comics writer Garth Ennis. I can't highlight enough what a bizarre combination that would have been. They were polar opposites of each other. Garth is a solid, down-to-earth, no-nonsense bloke from Belfast, who likes his steak, Guinness and pale ales. Art is a flouncey metrosexual urbanite. They were the proverbial odd-couple. Art was also a true blue Anglophile, to the point of obsessively watching *EastEnders* on cable—something that would come in useful in later life. Art already had his eye and heart set on London.

Meanwhile, I'd misguidedly still continued publishing *Tim True Stories*. Comics journalist Paul H. Birch reviewed it in the small press magazine, *Zum* in January 1992 calling it an "…excellent little anthology…[that] has all the right ingredients to become a monthly addiction." Which was lovely considering I had very little to do with it. I'd successfully ridden on the coattails of greater talents than I, and in doing so, started to realise that maybe my strengths lay, not in writing and drawing, or even colouring, but in editing and publishing.

A man I never met, Denis Grahame from Reading, sent me a strip featuring me for the comic. The slightly disturbing contents featured Tim True as a young boy discovering his first erection in the bath. He later explained in a letter that he didn't realise the character was based on a real person. Probably the "True" bit in the title confused him. To this day, I still don't know who Denis was. And it's probably best that way.

A year later and all the staff and regulars at Showcase had secretly produced a savage satire, *Tim False Stories*, behind my back. Here were friends, colleagues, regular customers, who'd put a lot of time and effort into parodying me and basically taking the piss. I didn't know whether to be flattered or insulted. I settled on a mix of both: bemused mock-indignation. I guess that's when Tim True became meta and separated from me and reality.

It was around this time that James decided to sell his house in Edmonton, and so me and Fiona Jerome (the other housemate) were forced to seek accommodation elsewhere. One of our regulars, who'd been rashly foolish enough to help me out on *Tim True*, said he had a spare room in Clapton Pond. Rather rashly I said "Great!" and moved in.

As a flatmate, "Pete Postie" AKA Count Libido, was excellent. Unfortunately, the flat wasn't. It was on the ground floor of a council block, and was secretly being sub-let to us by the real tenant, Mr Singh. I had the larger of two bedrooms, but it didn't have central heating, which meant it was cool and breezy in the summer and fucking freezing in the winter. Damp and condensation ran off the windows and walls for three months of the year. The neighbourhood was rough too. In fact, the only saving graces were that it was cheap, and there was a 24-hour bagel bakery around the corner. But Pete and I got on and we spent a lot of time putting together further issues of *Tim True*, photocopying, and physically cutting and pasting the pages up.

All this passion and misplaced dedication to the sequential art form brought me to the attention of cartoonist Brad Brooks, an equally misguided fool who felt that comics could change the world. Brad had work appearing in *Brain Damage* and *Gas* (alongside TV pundit, Charlie Brooker) and acted as UK correspondent for Fantagraphics' *The Comics Journal*, and we were both members of The Society of Strip Illustration (SSI)—with Brad actually on the committee for a period. Once a month we'd go down to The London Sketch Club in Chelsea and meet fellow comic "pros" (I was incognito) and discuss the issues of the day. The Sketch Club had been founded in 1898 and moved to its current location in 1957. The building had a heavily wood panelled interior with the bar and meeting room up two short flights of stairs. The silhouettes of past famous cartoonist members were painted on the wall of the main room and greats like Heath Robinson, H.M. Bateman and Phil May looked down on us comics lot disapprovingly. There was a distinctly old-fashioned and run-down air about the place.

Brad and I would often get there as the committee—which included Neil Gaiman, David Lloyd, Nick Vince, Win Wiacek (who I'd first met in Forbidden Planet six years previously), and others—was in session. So Brad and I would wait in the bar next door and chat. But, if the noise level got too loud so that we could be heard in the meeting, Pete Mastin—a six-foot five-inch lanky, bald geezer with tattoos, numerous piercings in both ears and anger management issues—would charge out of the meeting and scream in our faces to shut up. This happened more than once, and was a truly terrifying sight to behold. The SSI eventually morphed into the CCG (Comic Creators Guild) in 1993, after a long, agonising and tedious debate over the name change.

I think it was here that I first met New Zealand cartoonist Roger Langridge, through Brad. Brad was interested in starting up a comics collective inspired by French comics rather than American or British ones. We gathered a motley crew of three Brits (me, Brad and Tony Rooney) three Kiwis (Dylan Horrocks, Roger Langridge and Richard Bird) and a French woman (Sylvie Joly). Inspired by Bande Dessinée we called ourselves Les Cartoonistes Dangereux (pretentious, nous?). The plan was to produce an anthology and simultaneously publish it in English and French (with Sylvie providing translations).

We were all fans of Bande Dessinée and would regularly visit the French Bookshop in South Kensington to pick up the latest imports, as well as attending the numerous comic events Paul Gravett set up at the French embassy, round the corner.

We put together a small black and white A5 publication called *Le Roquet* (which was French slang for a small yappy dog, apparently) and bravely headed out to the western world's biggest comics festival, Angoulême, in France, on 23 January 1992.

Angoulême is a small medieval town on the banks of the Charente, just an hour's drive north of Bordeux. It has been the host of many festivals, including a popular jazz one, the Circuit des Ramparts (a vintage car race around the old town) and International Forum for Animation Technologies. But in 1974 they held the very first Festival International de la Bande Dessinée d'Angoulême. The festival was so popular it became an annual event, held during the last week in January.

The scale of the festival is mind-blowing. I was used to British comic conventions, where the most you'd get would be 5,000 people. Here, there were 50 times more than that. Over quarter of a million people! It is vast and encompasses the entire town, so that every shoe shop, chemist, patisserie and boulangerie has a comic-themed window display.

That year the guest country was America (the Brits having invaded two years before). On the train from Paris to Angoulême we met a young American inker, who, after several beers in the bar, asked, "So what part of Australia are you from?" We stared at him for a moment in disbelief and then realised he must've been joking. The previous month the long-running sitcom *Only Fools and Horses* had Del and Rodney going to America and constantly being mistaken for Aussies. So naturally we figured he was pulling our leg. "No, really, whereabouts in Australia do you live?" We were indignant: "We're bloody English!" we cried. "Can't you tell by our accents?" It turns out that Americans can no more discern an Aussie voice from a Brit one, than we can between a Yank and a Canuck.

That young artist was Rod Ramos, who went on to ink Warren Ellis and Darick Robertson's cult hit *Transmetropolitan* and far too many comics since to list. We've been friends for over 20 years now, and I never fail to bring his *faux pas* up.

Other attendees included Sergio Aragonés (technically Spanish/Mexican), Chester Brown, Colin Upton and Julie Doucet (technically all Canadians), Charles Burns, David Mazzucchelli and Kyle Baker. All were really lovely people and did sketches for me—Sergio's in a blur, living up to the moniker of the fastest cartoonist alive!

That year Robert Crumb had an exhibition of his work, and even performed a fantastic concert with his occasional band, Les Primitifs du Futur, the cartoonist plucking deftly away on his banjo. The following night we caught up with Aline Kominsky-Crumb, Robert's cartoonist wife, and Jesse, his son from a previous marriage, and we all ended up boogieing down to Mike Richardson and various Dark Horse-related staff and creators' rock and roll band.

Back home, the Les Cartoonistes crowd felt bolstered and enthused as we planned our next steps. The following month (February, 1992) a group of Americans planned to undermine UKCAC's UK convention monopoly and set up a show at Alexandra Palace in London and *Hellboy* creator Mike Mignola and Jim Lee were guests.

Unfortunately, I was stuck in the shop the whole weekend, so didn't actually get out to the con, but on the Saturday evening I'd managed to wangle a ticket to the hottest party in town, thanks to Dave Elliott, who was now the head of Tundra UK, a new publishing house set up the previous year.

Tundra had been established by Kevin Eastman, co-creator of the *Teenage Mutant Ninja Turtles*, who had literally made millions from the spin-off toys, animation show, movies and comics. His faith and love of comics saw him plough millions of dollars into the company to help struggling creators develop their comics and graphic novels. It was wonderfully philanthropic, and desperately naive. The sharks smelt money in the water and began to circle.

The Tundra party was held in the central hall of the Natural History Museum, Kensington. Lavish, extravagant, ostentatious, misguided. All of these words pale when trying to describe the event. Dave greeted everyone in a dinner jacket, burgundy-paisley bow tie, and a mullet—the haircut, not the fish. The free bubbly flowed. It was quite an experience to be sipping champagne while chatting to John and Liliana Bolton under the famous brachiosaurus skeleton after hours. Everyone who was anyone in British comics was there. Plus a few people who weren't, including me. The guest list ranged from Garth Ennis, John McCrea, Woodrow Phoenix, Jamie Hewlett, Glenn Fabry, and Dougie Braithwaite, to Paul Johnson, Matt "D'Israeli" Brooker, Garry Leach, Steve White, and Al Davison, who recalled fellow artist, "Melinda Gebbie's entrance in a black rubber evening gown, is hard to forget!"

When the bottles of bubbly ran dry at the museum, Tundra shipped everyone into two coaches and back to the main convention hotel bar, where the free booze continued. Then one-time *Deadline* editor, and Renaissance man, Frank Wynne settled down at the white grand piano and entertained us with a few numbers. The whole thing cost in excess of £10,000 (The equivalent of over £18,000 today). As then-editor of *Revolver*, Peter Hogan, recalled, "I'm still gobsmacked that you can have a party like that to celebrate... nothing!"

Seven months later and Tundra UK had gone through the fastest turnaround of fortunes. They had said yes to practically every project pitched to them, yet very few creators had actually delivered anything. There was a lot of brouhaha about how Tundra UK was going to save the British comics industry, but it was just so much "sound and fury, signifying nothing." There were rumours that they were haemorrhaging cash by Fed-Exing their dirty laundry back from Angoulême, and that lavish leather furniture meant for the office disappeared into senior management's homes. Things were so bad they had to make an announcement in the UKCAC '92 booklet stating, "Like Mister Twain, reports of our demise have been greatly exaggerated." The truth was that the brand had become so toxic that they re-labeled themselves as Atomeka, the company Dave Elliot and Garry Leach had originally set up to publish *A1*.

For the rest of the week, after the Alexandra Palace con, the very affable Mike Mignola hung around Showcase, mooching about, despite my protestations that he should go and explore the city. I never did understand that.

By now the Showcase staff had completely changed around since I'd started. J.B., Rube and Stick had all moved on, and we had a variety of new staff that rotated through, including Stretch, Hickey, Cliff, Don and Gianni—an Italian from Rome. One sunny lunch-time, while Paul H was at the other branch in Cambridge, Paul Gambaccini came in to Showcase, as usual, but unusually asked me out to lunch. He had a business proposal. I got Don to cover for me on the till and we popped into one of the numerous cafes dotted around.

Gambo said that he and Jonathan Ross were thinking of setting up their own comic shop and would I be interested in managing it for them. I was stunned, and sincerely flattered. I didn't know what to say, so asked for a few days to think about it. While I owed Paul H a hell of a lot, Paul G was offering me the chance to run my own shop the way I wanted. Jonathan was more of a silent partner, providing the majority of the backing. I think they secretly just wanted a clubhouse of their own that they could get their weekly comics easily and hang out in.

When we next met up I told Gambo "OK, count me in." After that we spent innumerate lunch breaks scouting round the West

End, looking for suitable locations for the shop. We looked at the Trocadero shopping centre in Piccadilly and many other sites. Over that period we became good friends, and I have Paul to thank for broadening my cultural horizons by taking me to my first classical concert at the Elizabeth Hall on the South Bank. To hear a complete orchestra in full tilt for the first time was utterly exhilarating.

After several months of location scouting we finally discovered a smallholding in St. Anne's Court, a small pedestrian alleyway that connected Wardour Street to Dean Street, in the heart of Soho. It was in almost exactly the same location as the final resting place of Dark They Were and Golden Eyed, which seemed portentous at the time. Paul and Jonathan snatched it up.

But then another golden opportunity hit the fan.

Marvel UK were looking for an assistant editor. I had many friends who were working at the publisher, either on-staff or as freelancers, including Steve White, Steve Whittaker, Nick Abadzis, Edmund Perryman, Simon Jowett and Charlie Adlard.

Editor Steve White knew I was looking to break into comics and had put in a good word for me, so I went down to their gothic, red brick offices at Arundel House, Arundel Street, next to Temple tube station, and met with Paul Neary, Marvel UK's Editor-in-Chief. Over a brief pub lunch, we discussed the job, my experience and comics in general. No promises were made, but nothing was ruled out either. It was looking hopeful. Marvel UK had been expanding massively, launching a whole range of very successful US-sized comic books including *Death's Head II*, *Hell's Angel*, *Warheads*, *Digitek* and *Motormouth*, which would make stars out of artists Liam Sharp, Bryan Hitch, Gary Erskine and many others.

I returned to Showcase after my lunchbreak beaming, but unable to explain the reason why. I now had two potential job offers.

Then, golden opportunity three hit the fan.

Art Young was looking for an assistant editor to join him in his new London Vertigo office, and he asked if I was interested.

This was crazy. They say ceramic ducks, celebrity deaths at Christmas and chances come in threes. All of a sudden I had a trio of potentially major, life-changing jobs on the horizon. My dream was coming true. It had taken me four and a half years, but I was finally going to get a job in comic book publishing.

It was a no-brainer where I'd end up, really. The choice of carrying on working in retail (albeit managing the shop for two famous TV celebs, Gambo & Wossy) didn't hold much appeal. And frankly, with a few exceptions, I was never that into what Marvel UK were publishing. In an interview that was more a formality than anything else, I said "yes" to Art as casually as I could without blowing my cool. Which wasn't easy.

There were plenty of people in the UK who were perfectly more qualified for the Vertigo Assistant Editor's job than I—working at *Deadline*, Fleetway, Marvel UK and the like—and I know many applied. But Art didn't want someone who'd learnt the ropes from another publisher and who he'd have to re-train. He wanted a protégé he could mould in his own likeness. Paradoxically, my complete lack of professional work as an editor proved to be my strongest selling point. If I could put my finger on any particular reasons why I got the job it was probably down to being at the right place at the right time; understanding with a passion what Vertigo was trying to do; and most importantly, understanding Art, and where he was coming from. That, and my boyish good looks.

I made my apologies to Gambo, who was quite rightly upset, and I felt bad that I'd left them in the lurch, somewhat. The Marvel job never quite materialised in the end, so there was nothing to say there. And so I finally had to let Paul Hudson know that I was handing in my notice.

By the time I left Comic Showcase there were only two original members of staff left from when I'd started; Paul and myself. I'd begun there as a means to get a foot in the door in comics publishing. At the time I figured it would take a year or two. It turned out to be almost half a decade. But it had worked. I was going to work for my favourite publisher, in the hippest part of town, with the coolest guy I knew. Little did I know how low this insalubrious career would take me. And, by the time it was all over, what depths of depravity I would have sunk to...

CHAPTER THREE
DIZZY HEIGHTS...

"It would take days to catalog your sins…
I simply don't have the time."

—Sebastian O, Grant Morrison & Steve Yeowell

The Warner Brothers building at 135-141 Wardour Street was an impressive seven-floor Art deco building erected in 1932 by James J S Naylor. The entrance was right on the corner of Berwick Street and Wardour Street, slap bang in the centre of Soho's film industry.

The ground floor was occupied by "Consumer Products," the licensing department who were responsible for all the Batman slippers, Bugs Bunny mugs, Daffy Duck T-shirts and Superman pyjamas in the UK. The next two floors were full of sales managers dealing with movie distribution and cinemas. Above them was the large accounts department. Finally, on the top floor, was the press office, the Managing Director, Maj-Britt's office, and the Vertigo UK secret lair.

The Vertigo office was quite spacious. As you walked in the door, my desk was to the left, tucked into a corner. Straight ahead, facing the door was Art's desk, which permanently had two chairs in front of it for the endless visitors who'd drop by. To the right of Art's desk was a large round table with four chairs, which was barely used, apart from as a storage dump. The rest of the furniture, all in "bachelor black," consisted of two cupboards (keeping multiple copies of all our comics), a large flat chest storing the original artwork, and a couple of filing cabinets, on top of which sat a fax machine—our lifeline to New York and our freelancers in this pre-Internet age. In fact, for the first couple of months we had to cope with electric typewriters because, as Society of Young Publishers' magazine, *In Print*, reported, "The office is so new their computers haven't even caught up with them."

Behind Art, on some white shelves, sat copies of all the titles he'd edited at Vertigo along with a few DC superhero action figures, including gay-friendly icon Aquaman (AKA Arthur Curry). Plus, his favourite *New Yorker* cartoon, by Robert Mankoff, of a man in an office on the phone, checking his diary: "No, Thursday's out. How about never—is never good for you?" That perfectly encapsulated Art's sense of humour—wry and acerbic.

Because of the time difference and need to be in frequent contact with the New York office we worked unusual hours. Our average day started at 11am and finished at 8pm in the UK. This meant that, with New York's five hour delay, we had a full six hours in which we could talk to everyone we needed to—such as Production, Karen Berger and Legal—between 9am-3pm EST. This suited our—as I was soon to discover—hedonistic lifestyle perfectly. 8pm was just the right time in the evening to go straight out to drinks in Soho, but 11am was a late enough start in the morning to recover enough from the previous night's excesses.

As a gay man recently self-outed, Soho was like Disneyland to Art. The bright sparkly neon signs, the lithe, ripped bodies, and pumping house music all promised untold, thrilling rides. He was "on constant lookout for wood nymphs"—svelte young men to satisfy his carnal desires.

But behind this public persona of a happy-go-lucky-sexual-predator, he actually just wanted to find a nice normal guy to settle down with. Unfortunately, nine times out of 10, most of the guys he attracted, or was attracted to, turned out to be flaky losers, or psychos. It was a perennial source of concern for him, and I quickly grasped that my Assistant Editor duties also involved becoming Art's confidant, as I listened to his many woes, like some overly dramatic soap opera.

Art gave me the nickname "Boychik," which I mistakenly took as some sort of gay epithet, but was in fact Yiddish in origin.

My training began by learning what Grant Morrison described as "the distinctly louche editing [style] of Arthur Young". Firstly, when editing scripts, there were the standard technical issues of spelling, grammar, syntax and punctuation. Obviously, being an American company, we had to Americanise any spelling or colloquialisms, from our British writers. But editing is about much more than simply making sure the spelling is correct. It's a process of working with the writer to develop the protagonists' voices and actions, ensuring that they remain true to character throughout the story. And the story itself has to be comprehendible. Often writers would be so immersed in the story that they would forget to make something that should be blindingly obvious, actually clear to the reader.

So this would often involve several discussions with the writer, negotiating certain use of words, figuring out the pacing of the story, making sure the art directions in the panel descriptions were clear enough for the artist, etc. Art tenaciously hung on to this aspect of the process, as it was the most creative, and fun, part of the job.

Once the script had been edited it was sent to the artist, who would produce rough thumbnail breakdowns of each page. Once these were approved, they'd pencil up the full-size pages.

Art then introduced me to the ancient and mysterious art of "ballooning-up." This wasn't some sort of anaphylactic reaction, but rather the process for guiding the letterer. Not every editor did this, but Art was very pro-active and hands-on about it. After editing the script he'd number all the text and dialogue and then draw corresponding speech balloons and caption boxes on the original art in non-repro blue pencil. If the artwork was fully painted, I'd make A3 photocopies and Art would mark these up. I did a LOT of photocopying in those days.

The reason for doing this was that Art felt that the speech and caption boxes were an integral part of the overall design of the page and how they were laid out affected the way the eye flowed across the artwork from top to bottom, left to right. Obviously letterers couldn't be trusted with such an important task, so it was laid out for them, by us. I was an ardent believer in this and have turned from a ballooning acolyte to fervent preacher over the years.

The ballooned-up pencil pages would then go to the letterer, who would either letter straight onto the original artwork, or on an overlay in the case of painted art. Often, when comic book writers tell the unacquainted their job title, many assume it's the letterer's role they are talking about, "Oh, you write all the little speech balloons?"

The pencilled and lettered artwork would then be returned to the artist for inking. Finally, we'd send photocopies or bluelines out to the colourist. Being the final link in the chain, the colourist always gets the shitty end of the stick in the comic book production line. If a book was running late, and they invariably did, it was up to the poor colourist to make up the lost time. The shorter the deadline the faster they'd have to work, and at no extra cost. A colourist's lot is not a happy one, and in many ways I was quite glad I never pursued this particular career avenue any more than I did.

I was on a probationary period and consequently, for the first three months, I didn't get any credits in the books, despite having worked on the last four issues of *Enigma* (By Peter Milligan and Duncan Fegredo), and the last issue of *Sebastian O* (By Grant Morrison and Steve Yeowell). So it was a real buzz to finally see my first official DC Comics credit in print in *The Extremist* #1. Written by Peter Milligan and drawn by Ted McKeever, *The Extremist* was at least 10 years ahead of its time. Art described it—and, quite possibly, our lifestyle—as "A no holds-barred look at pushing life to dangerous limits." It discussed the nature of sex, sexuality and moral ambiguity without being titillating. No mean feat. Pete's clever use of jumping around the timeline made for some excellently complex cliffhangers and Ted's art was just sublime.

It was the first title where I felt I made small, but significant, contributions. In the first few years of Vertigo, all the covers had a margin "banner" running down the left hand side. What was done with this was up to the editorial and design teams. Art had already come up with the idea of a large zip filling the margin, tying in with the bondage and S&M theme, but I suggested the zip could get lower with each issue revealing a flesh colour underneath. The other part was the end of issue two, which is partly narrated by the audio tapes of the main protagonist's husband. The original dialogue ran "…I think this tape is about to run out" but I suggested that the dialogue cut off in mid-sentence to add an air of authenticity. Ted very kindly gave me the original artwork of that page, which I still treasure. As I said, infinitesimal contributions, but it made me feel as if I was being listened to and my ideas were taken seriously and acted upon. This is what editing was all about. Collaborating, working in a team to develop the best possible creative outcome. Ted even faxed us a little trio of cartoon heads of Art, Ted and Tim, which read underneath "Fun Boy 3!"

Surprisingly, considering the distinctly racy themes in the series, we rarely came across any censorship, except for one instance. As Ted recalled, "In Pete's script he says, 'Have a sex club where everyone's having sex.' So I drew it, and DC's going, 'Wait a minute! You can't show *that* sex!' I'm like, 'Okay, let me back up a little bit. How about *this* sex? How's that?' They said, 'Okay, that's much better!'" The scene Ted was describing was a sex club orgy, but was drawn very tastefully, with couples semi-clothed, or partially hidden in shadows.

However, there was one very prominent couple that were doing it doggy-style and the lawyers panicked, fearing "*that* sex!" would be misinterpreted as anal, revealing that DC's legal team had somewhat limited experience of various sexual positions.

I finally caught up with Ted, at the 2010 New York Comic Con, after a decade and a half of being out of touch, and we discussed doing a deluxe collected hardcover version with extra sketches and background material. The book was creator-owned and it hadn't been in print for over a decade—despite Ted approaching them a couple of times—so technically he and Pete had the right to shop it around to other publishers. Unfortunately, this never came to pass, but I always felt the series deserved to be one of those important graphic novels that people talk about. In exactly the same way they don't about *Face* (Milligan and Fegredo's true masterpiece).

Years later I was gutted to see DC Comics released a collected version of *The Extremist* under their *Vertigo Resurrected* banner. It was so obviously cobbled together purely so DC could retain the publishing rights. The format was just a thick comic (100 pages) with cheap quality cover (less than 200gsm, for all you publishing nerds out there); they only reprinted one cover; and lost all the beautiful design panache that Ted and letterer John Costanza had put into the original series. Plus, there are no natural breaks in the storytelling, making the whole collection unnecessarily complicated. In the original miniseries, the story's timeline jumps backwards and forwards between issues, but you'd never know that from the collection, as the front pieces with the dates on had been removed, making the story-telling difficult to follow. Oh, and my credit line had been removed.

Vertigo UK's location—tucked right at the back of the top floor next to the 30-seater screening cinema and opposite the kitchen/bar—was extremely advantageous, as whenever there was an advanced screening of a Warner Bros.' film, we'd grab a beer from the bar and sneak in and watch.

Famous faces frequently swept past our always-open door on the way to the cinema. Film critic Barry Norman was a regular sight, as he didn't like to go to screenings with other journalists, and had enough clout with his BBC show, *Film 19-whatever-year-it-was*, that he could arrange private viewings. Once, film director Joel Schumacher popped his head in to use my phone. He reminded me of an older, greyer version of Art. If only I'd known what he'd had in store for the appalling Batman movie franchise in the successive years, I would've changed cinematic history by introducing his throat to my phone cable. But it was not to be.

Literally on the next block over from the Warner Bros. building, in St. Anne's Court, was Paul Gambaccini and Jonathan Ross' new comic shop, the prosaically named Top Ten Soho—the same shop I'd turned down the opportunity to run. The shop had a chart of the top 10 bestselling comics that week on the wall, hence the name. Paul and Jonathan had found a replacement manager for me in the guise of diminutive blonde punk Zoe, who had previously worked at Forbidden Planet, and she brought with her fellow co-worker Karl. The shop was small and long, and with hindsight I'd never have picked that location. It was tucked down a pedestrian alley, making it hard to find, with very little passing trade. This became our default comic shop, by the sheer locale. However, my allegiance to Comic Showcase meant that, more often than not, I'd take the 10-minute walk over there, rather than the 30-second one to Top Ten.

Art and I soon made friends with several people in the Warner Bros offices; Steve and Panchea from Accounts, Michael, Niamh and Richard in Licensing, and Jane from Sales, and these formed our nucleus. This was our "gang". We hung out together at every opportunity that wasn't taken up hanging out with comics creators. In the summer we played softball in Green Park every Thursday and finished off the matches with drinks and falafels outside Ye Grapes pub in Shepherd Market, in the heart of the notorious, upmarket Mayfair red light district. It was here that Mama Cass of The Mamas and Papas and The Who's Keith Moon died four years apart. It was at these softball matches that I got to know two Australians, James and Michael, who were living in Notting Hill in West London. They would prove to be my saviour from the mean streets of Clapton Pond.

Having gotten to know James and Michael, Jane, Niamh and I started hanging out in Notting Hill and drinking around there. Favourite haunts included Beach Blanket Babylon, The Market Bar, The Ground Floor, the terminally hip Westbourne, The Cow (both later immortalised in Glyn Dillon's award-winning graphic novel, *The Nao of Brown*), and The Globe. This last one was our favourite drinking hole. Back in the archaic days before 24-hour drinking licenses in the UK, this was the only place you could get a drink in Notting Hill after 11pm. It had no windows and a large metal door. You had to ring a buzzer and a large Rastafarian opened the door, sized you up and let you in—if you knew what you were doing—and you paid three quid. Upstairs was pretty empty, but in the basement was where it was at—an illegal drinking den swathed in ganja smoke. There were red vinyl booths to sit in, once you'd bought a can of Red Stripe lager and made your way over the sticky, black and white chequered linoleum floor. The Globe, like all of Notting Hill at the time, had an edge (in a good way), but was friendly and egalitarian as well. All were welcome here from movie stars to shifty dealers.

After many a night out and faced with the over-an-hour-long trek back east, across London to Clapton, I frequently optioned for crashing on James and Michael's living room floor. When they moved to a larger three-bedroom flat at 52 Leamington Road Villas they offered me the spare room. I leapt at the chance to escape the down-at-heels, edgy (in a bad way)—and frankly, downright scary at times—Clapton Pond. I know it's very hip and gentrified now, but back then Hackney was the gun capital of London and dodgy as fuck.

So I moved across the city, westwards and upwards, into the trendy part of town. The flat was at the top of an end of terrace row, up five flights of stairs. Once inside there were another three flights to get to the living room and kitchen. We were right at the very top of the six-story building that was owned by three brothers who'd been given it by their Ukrainian father, Joe. Peter lived in the ground floor and basement, the middle brother rented out the middle flat and our landlord was Michael, the youngest son. Joe lived in another building that he owned, opposite. He was a stocky, bald man and would often do small repairs on our flat and frequent conversations would go:

Me: Would you like cup of coffee?

Joe: No no no.

Me: Tea?

Joe: No no.

Me: Er... Vodka?

Joe: Ahah!

Regardless of the time of day.

Next door, at No. 54, was an imposing detached three-story gothic house that had been split into two large properties. Our neighbours were Tory MP Lord Heseltine's daughter and journalist, Annabel, and the novelist Martin Amis. More often than not, on those long hot summer evenings, I'd lean out my bedroom window listening to the opera-singing neighbour to my right—blasting out arias that carried down the street—and see Amis on his kitchen balcony scribbling away on my left.

I decided that I should actually read some of my neighbour's output and picked up his *Einstein's Monsters* anthology. In the tragically disturbing, yet strangely redemptive, *Bujak and the Strong Force* I read about the eponymous character, who was an ex-circus strong man from Poland. As I mused on the description of this "Huge man, with massive fists and a hulking build" I started to realize that he bore striking resemblance to Joe. I mentioned this to his son, Peter, "I think this sounds a lot like your dad," I said, lending him my copy of the book. "See what you think."

A few weeks later we bumped into each other in the hallway.

Peter said, "I thought you were right, so asked Amis if he'd based the character on my dad. And he said yes, 'But for God's sake don't tell him!'" The entire story was based on Amis' observations of his neighbour, Joe, who he watched from his tiny balcony every day.

Having settled into Leamington Road Villas I was introduced to a succession of Aussies who either crashed at ours and were passing through, or were local ex-pat friends of James and Michael's. One of the latter was Bill, an amiable, stocky fella with the build and intellect of a rugby player. Bill's "hilarious" antics were far too numerous to mention—such as almost setting fire to our flat by leaving the iron on face down—but they provided an endless source of amusement to the Les Cartoonistes… gang. So much so that they became the basis for Roger Langridge's *Bill the Clown* mini-comic. When he discovered there already existed a *Bill the Clown* comic he changed the name to Fred and it became one of the first one-shot comics LCD published. *Fred the Clown* went on to have a successful life at Fantagraphics, gaining Roger two Eisner, a Harvey, a Reuben and two Ignatz Award nominations.

Back at the office, the days whizzed by, as I learnt the ropes. April rolled around, and with it came GlasCAC (the Glasgow Comic Art Convention), the tartan-clad cousin of UKCAC. We flew up to Scotland on the Friday and checked into the Copthorne hotel on George Square, joining fellow Vertigo editor Stuart Moore, who was over from New York.

On the Saturday night Art, Stuart, and I took some freelancers out to the best Chinese restaurant in Glasgow, Ho Wong. The seven of us sat around a huge circular table. Here I was having dinner with Peter Milligan, Grant Morrison, Jamie Delano, and Dick Foreman, four of Vertigo's biggest writers at the time. This was it. I had entered the inner sanctum that all fanboys dream of! Having dinner with my favourite comic book scribes. All had fearsome reputations and I was terrified of making a *faux pas*, so sat as passively as possible, smiling and watching every word I said.

Milligan had classic matinee idol looks. A chiselled façade and coiffured hair, which was a source of much discussion amongst himself. It was foppish, short back and sides and long on top. Sans the hair gel, it was a quiff-in-waiting. He wasn't so much vain as, just acutely, crystal clearly, self-aware. He was a handsome bastard, and he knew it.

There was very little, barely a trace, in fact nothing, to betray his second-generation working class Irish/London roots. His rapier wit flashed with glinting steel over any dark conversation and he often spoke deliberately in double negatives, a not entirely unappealing trait. "Fucking Jesus!" he'd often exclaim, with a schoolboy's cheeky grin. When asked, "Are you meeting Karen Berger?" at one UKCAC, he quipped, "Mmm. Dinner first. Maybe sex later." Like all writers, he was a perpetual magpie, stealing snippets of conversation and turns of phrase that would appear six months later in printed form in a script on my desk. You had to be careful what you said around him, he was a living tape recorder.

His acerbic wit and sharp turn of phrase led artist and long-time collaborator Brett Ewins to call Milligan the "Anthony Burgess of comics" but I prefer to think of him as "the Martin Amis of comics". However, I suspect Milligan sees himself as the "Peter Milligan of comics." If Art had a single best mate, Milligan was it.

Morrison, meanwhile, had wispy dark hair, an impossibly skinny body and the softest Glaswegian accent I have ever heard. He could be cruelly caustic at times and he scared me just a little bit.

Morrison and Milligan were cut from similar cloth. Both had a love of the absurd and had bonded sometime beforehand over screwdrivers (the drink, not the tool), hashish and the decadent lifestyle comics afforded them. They were young, handsome, fêted and rich(ish) and they were going to enjoy it for as long as it lasted.

Delano, on the other hand, was the perfect poker player, his cards firmly placed on his chest. He never spoke if it didn't warrant it, but when he did it was often droll, biting satire, like lemon juice in a cut. He was from Northampton and had the same laconic drawl and drawn-out elongated speech as Alan Moore and a seemingly similar dour demeanour, which was just a front. Delano's intellect was equal to that of Moore and was tempered with a seemingly embittered hatred for all of humanity. Or rather, more fairly, an utter dismay at the vast majority of human beings and their self-destructive manner. His humour made the Kalahari Desert seem like a swimming pool. A former minicab driver turned writer he constantly smoked rollies (a very uncool thing back in the day when cigarettes were cheap) and was a staunch socialist. His short faintly reddish hair, goatee and large glasses and black leather jacket gave him a formidable appearance, like a bouncer.

Dick was much quieter than the others, I seem to recall, content to watch Milligan and Morrison hold court. I always got the feeling that the slightly balding scribe seemed a tad bemused to be where he was, writing a major title, *Black Orchid* (which had been revamped by Gaiman and McKean earlier) for Vertigo. A feeling I could completely empathise with.

Stuart Moore was a short New York Jew with glasses, which describes just about every single person I know in American publishing. He wasn't as bombastic as Art (*no one* was as bombastic as Art), and like Dick, he kept fairly quiet, letting Art and the other writers do most of the talking—just inserting the right witty gem occasionally. I followed suit by keeping my mouth shut.

As the meal wrapped up Milligan declined the proffered selection of brie, cheddar and stilton, "I don't eat cheese. It's dead milk," he quipped.

My first writing for DC's in-house newsletter, *Shop Talk*, reported on GlasCAC '93 and was full of euphemisms. I'd learnt pretty quickly that most Americans hadn't grasped the fact that 90% of UK comic business is done over a pint or 10, so I had to use discretion when describing what we'd been up to. Therefore, when I described the weekend event as the "professional's convention" that actually meant there were very few attendees and it was just an excuse for the professionals to get together and have a piss-up (more so), without being bothered by too many fans. And when I pointed out that the *Hellblazer* team of Garth Ennis and Steve Dillon were burning "the midnight oil into the wee small hours, obviously getting more research done for their next issue" I really meant they were propping up the bar and drinking the EU Guinness lake dry.

Across the whole comics industry at the time the expenses were legendary. And Vertigo UK was no exception. There wasn't a restaurant in Soho we hadn't taken a freelancer to, either to thank them for a job well done, to wine and dine them to get them to work for us, or simply because we needed an excuse to go to a new restaurant that had just opened. We ate well, and frequently. Favourite haunts included the French House; the over-priced pizza joint Kettners (which had its own in-house pianist); and L'Epicurian, a traditional French restaurant where at least four elderly waiters served every table simultaneously. Their staff overheads must've been astronomical, and were reflected in the prices. Keeping it old school, they brought the raw meat out for you to choose your cut and then preceded to flambé it in front of you. Then there was The Groucho, Soho House, Atlantic, Titanic... The list was endless.

Having returned from Scotland in a typically jaded state I received our monthly package of DC trade paperbacks and comics from the New York office. *Justice League of America* #75 (cover dated June 1993) made it official. On the last page, in the DC Universe section under DC Bullets it read: "Art Young, one of our VERTIGO editors in England, has just welcomed aboard a new assistant! Tim Pilcher will be keeping Art company all those gruelling hours hanging out with our overseas chaps like Grant Morrison, Peter Milligan and Duncan Fegredo." This was the first time my name had appeared in a DC comic. I was ecstatic. Not only that, but I was the very first British member of DC's editorial staff in its 56-year history.

It was Thursday afternoon and the weekend was looming once more, so Art made his usual phone call to "Dodgy Andy."

"Andy? Hi. Yeah. Good, thanks. Listen can you drop off 15 T-shirts later on? Yeah? Cool? Half an hour? Grreeat." His Septic accent drawled.

"Dodgy Andy" was Art's dealer. The "T-shirts" were Ecstasy tablets and Art dished them out like a philanthropic, psychedelic Easter Bunny. Andy also supplied coke on a semi-regular basis—the real thing, not the fizzy kind.

Art revelled in being a siren, luring young, impressionable artists and writers onto the rocks of disrepute. "Listen, the only difference between a straight guy and a gay guy is a six pack of beer or an Ecstasy pill," was one of his many semi-jokey phrases. I'm sure that there were many British comic creators who fell victim to his wily, seductive charms and little white pills.

It was not without some irony that Art wrote in an *On The Ledge* guest editorial in all of November, 1994's Vertigo titles, "Most of you are probably unaware of what goes on in DC's London office". I'm sure if Warner Brothers and DC had been aware of what had gone on, and discovered how many drugs were being passed through their offices they would have freaked.

"Dodgy Andy" was such a frequent visitor to our offices, and a renowned member of the Vertigo UK clique, that he even made a guest appearance in Grant Morrison and Philip Bond's *Kill Your Boyfriend* on Page 24 Panel 4 where the huge neon-pink nightclub sign bore his *nom de drogue*.

Morrison later recalled in his book, *Supergods*, that the Vertigo office was "a glittering mirror-ball where the future of comics was cooked and served by cackling pranksters on shiny chemicals." And "…when Art Young was running the short-lived, fondly-remembered,

London office of Vertigo as a 24-hour gay acid disco." Our unspoken mantra (we had a lot of mantras) was the Wildean, "Nothing succeeds like excess."

In the same *On The Ledge* column that he practically confessed to our excessive drug taking, Art wrote, "But rest assured the PR agency of Young & Pilcher will also continue trying to get Vertigo's (and DC's) finest out there and into the hearts and minds of unsuspecting Britons." This meant me pulling the short straw five months earlier, and having to go on primetime *Sky News* to talk about Batman. It was the time of the epic *Knightfall* saga that ran in *Batman* and *Detective Comics*, when The Dark Knight is broken (both mentally and physically) when the villain Bane snaps Bruce Wayne's spine in half. This went on to form the basis of Christopher Nolan's third, woeful, Batman film, *The Dark Knight Rises*.

At the time, Batparaplegic was big "news", and so Sky sent a car to pick me up from the office and drive me to the studio as a representative of DC Comics. I'd only been with the company four months! I was nervous as hell as I sat behind the desk, sweating under the studio lights on an already hot day in June. Typically, *Sky News*, like all pernicious media, had their own agenda, "So Batman breaking his back. Isn't that a bit violent for a children's comic?' I patiently explained that the target audience for most comics these days were in the 16-24 year-old age bracket. "But a character like Batman is best known as a children's character. Aren't you worried you'll upset parents?" I pointed out that various precedents for adult-themed Batman stories had already been set, including Frank Miller's *The Dark Knight Returns*. "Just coming back to the violence for a moment…" And so this circular conversation repeated itself for a full five minutes (which felt like five hours) before they ran out of time, the producer thanked me and I was bundled back into a car to the West End. In the quarter of a century I've spent talking to the press I've met less than five mainstream journalists that really understood comics, and even then their stories were ruined by crass and ignorant editors or producers.

Steve from the Warner Brothers accounts department was having a party at his that night. Kristen (AKA "Bubbles") met us in the pub and we headed over to Steve's in Clapham. When we arrived Michael, Niamh, Jane and Panchea were already there. The latter three were making hash brownies. We stood on Steve's terrace and watched the summer sun set over London, while the girls presented their culinary attempts. Unfortunately none of them were exactly Nigella Lawsons (in the kitchen at least) and the resultant mess on the baking trays resembled more a morass of chocolaty goo than actual brownies. Never-the-less we scooped the drug-laden sweet mess up with our fingers and consumed the lot with wild, reckless abandon. None of us had eaten cannabis before, so were unprepared for what happened next.

As cocktails and joints were being passed around, the darkness continued to grow and the temperature started to drop, so several of the party withdrew to the living room. I brassed out the balcony as long as possible and eventually succumbed and made my way to the sofa. I sat down and feeling drowsy, started to lose the thread of the conversations. I closed my eyes, just for a moment, and let the dark warmth wash over me.

When I opened my eyes, I was on the floor and it was daylight and 12 hours later. All around me were bodies strewn about on chairs, sofas and the floor. Not everyone had crashed, but a large portion of the party had passed out pretty much where I remembered them.

That taught us all an important lesson. If you're going to eat cannabis, go slow. It takes twice as long to kick in and hits you four times as hard. It was a bitter lesson my mate Cheeky was to find out at another party. One that I felt embarrassingly responsible for.

The following Friday David Hine popped into the office late in the afternoon to discuss his series *Strange Embrace* that was looking for a new home after the Tundra debacle. His excellent creator-owned dark horror story was perfect for our little corner of Vertigo and we suggested continuing the meeting in The Ship over the road. David was unsure about the professionalism of carrying on a discussion—that had already lasted two hours in the office without even getting to the topic at hand—down the pub over booze.

"It'll be fine," Art reassured him, "I'm always at work, thanks to Mr. Mobile Phone."

The Ship pub was our refuge. Literally 20 feet across the road, it became our spiritual hangout and haunt after work. We became such regulars, we were on first name terms with all the staff and management, a rare thing in a West End pub. The Ship was essentially a pre-clubbing pub, it would be packed between 6-10 and then suddenly empty as everyone scattered to the many nightspots in the area. It was also the birthplace of Underworld's *Born Slippy*, as Karl Hyde and Bill Bailey regularly drank there and the latter inspired the former to write the music that would become a soundtrack for a generation.

The pints began flowing freely as industry gossip took hold of the conversation. A few pints more and Art disappeared to the toilet to powder his nose. He returned distinctly more animated, slipped me a small paper envelope and I repeated the process. Poor David was stuck the whole night in the pub with two coked-up buffoons telling him how great he was and how we were definitely going to publish the collected colour edition of *Strange Embrace*.

"Definitely?" asked David, incredulously.

"Definitely," Said Art.

"Definitely," I added, wiping my sniffles.

"Definitely," Art confirmed.

Did we publish it?

Did we fuck.

On Monday I opened up the daily Fed Ex box. It was usually either artwork from our creators or packs from the New York office. This one was the latter. In it were a few advance copies of *Sebastian O #3* and the best piece of stationery I'd ever seen. A fanboy shudder ran through me as I held up an A5 blank notepad. At the top was the familiar DC "bullet" logo in royal blue. At the bottom it read "Tim Pilcher (071) 465-4279" I was now working for the best comic company in the world. The comic company I'd grown up reading. The home of the greatest superheroes on the planet, Superman, Batman and Wonder Woman. I had my own personalised notepad to prove it. I'd "made it."

I was still basking in this glow when Art burst into the office with a smile on his face and his usual first *Absolutely Fabulous* quote of the day, "OK, don't panic! Don't panic! I'm here now!"

I'd already been in an hour and a half, as I liked to get a good start on the day, usually by reading some of the many series proposals that flooded in. The perennially tall stack of submissions on my desk constantly nagged at me like some attention-deficient toddler. No matter how much I got through, the same amount would turn up the next day in the post. It was the editorial equivalent of painting the Forth Bridge. An unrelenting job that permanently resided in my "To do" lists. My job was supposedly to shift through the dross and seek out the gems to bring to Art's attention. But no matter how hard I championed any titles, he never picked up on my suggestions, even when it was a quality project like Ian Edginton and Matt Brooker's *Kingdom of the Wicked* (which had failed to be published by Atomeka and Tundra). Fortunately, it managed to find homes at Calibre (in black and white) and Dark Horse (rightly, in full colour), where it did very well. A lot of people who submitted stuff back then have since gone on to become professional creators and personal friends, like writers Robbie Morrison (no relation to Grant) and Martin Conaghan, and artists Rob McCallum and Chris McLaughlin. The problem was Art had his favourite creators (Milligan, Morrison, Fegredo, etc.) and he wasn't really interested in anyone he hadn't personally discovered.

What Vertigo actually was, and what it stood for, was always a bit of an enigma. The one question I was asked more than any other, by aspiring creatives, was "What sort of stories and material are you looking for?" and the completely unhelpful reply was always "We'll know it when we see it." But the truth was that we didn't want to pigeonhole ourselves to one genre or theme. We often joked that each story was "blah blah blah, but with a Vertigo twist" which was equally ambiguous. We had stories about superheroes, weird psychedelic tales, conspiracy adventures, horror, sci-fi. It really didn't matter, provided the content was quality and challenging to both the reader and the medium. A good example of how impossible it was to pin down the Vertigo publishing plan was the obscure tagline "Ideas in motion, remain in motion." I'm not sure who came up with the line, I think it was Karen, or even what the hell it actually means, but it ended up on a T-Shirt I still occasionally wear when decorating. Other bizarre taglines included "Listen Between the Lines" and

"Collect experiences. Speculate on ideas." None of them expressed my experience of Vertigo. "Weird shit to fuck with your head" would've been more appropriate.

One title that fitted that description perfectly was *Rogan Gosh* by Brendan McCarthy and Peter Milligan. Inspired by Brendan's love of Amar Chitra Katha Indian comics, which recounted classic mythologies like the *Ramayana* and *Mahabharata*, *Rogan Gosh* (named after a curry) was originally serialised in the short-lived *Revolver* anthology back in July 1990. We collected and repackaged the whole thing in a prestige format one-shot with additional material. It was a psychedelic trip through the mind of Rudyard Kipling via an Indian restaurant in Stoke Newington and on into the Karmanaut populated future. Or was it? It opened my eyes to the world of the sub-continent's sequential arts, and helped nurture a life-long obsession with the country and its culture.

I'd first met Jamie Hewlett, Alan Martin, Philip Bond, Glyn Dillon, and the rest of the *Deadline* crew in the bar at UKCAC in 1988. Inevitably, Art was also drawn to this gaggle of handsome, young creators and we spent many weekends down in Worthing, a small sleepy English town on the south coast known as "God's waiting room" on the account of the large elderly population. We'd hang out with the gang in the town's finest ice cream parlour/cafe, Macaris, and I still blame Hewlett for introducing me to Banoffie Pie and creating an ongoing addiction.

While the days were spent hanging out at the boys' various houses, pubs and seafront, the nights were spent in The Factory, Worthing's best nightclub (there were only two). The Factory (31, Chatsworth

Road) was the focal point for the arty Worthing scene. At the top of a long flight of stairs was one large shell of a room with a long bar at one end, and a raised dancefloor/stage with a DJ booth at the other. The sweat dripped off the black walls and grim Lynx lager was just a £1 a can, while the more elite bought Red Stripe for £1.50.

Jamie, Glyn and Philip decorated the walls with an assortment of original paintings ranging from Hewlett's "Da Groovy Goggle Gang" and Bond's fire-breathing Godzilla, to Dillon's giant reproductions of Seventies' *Star Wars* trading cards. Consequently, they had free admission whenever they wanted as payment, and abused this privilege with impunity.

The Factory was unique in that it was the very antithesis of "mainstream" clubs, playing gothic industrial, The Doors, mixed with the Madchester sound and a bit of Indie Pop thrown in. When we were down for Glyn's birthday he received a pre-release copy of Blur's *Modern Life is Rubbish*. He took it to The Factory that night and the DJ played the title track incessantly while Glyn merrily twirled on the dancefloor.

When the Factory eventually shut down, the new owners renamed it the Q Club and sacrilegiously painted over the original murals. However, there are rumours that they survive under chipboard, waiting to be discovered 300 years from now by pop culture archeologists.

Jamie married his first wife, the gorgeous Pippa, around that time, a stunning beauty who was a doppelganger for a young Michelle Pfeiffer—both of whom I harboured unrequited crushes on for years.

Having finally completed my probation period successfully, without burning the office down, DC made the very astute and wise move to send me to New York for a week in September 1993, so I could see the DC office, get to meet everyone and get to grips with the running of things. I was over the moon!

DC, at the time, was based at 1325 Avenue of the Americas, in midtown Manhattan, and they put me up in the Sheraton New York Hotel and Towers, over the road. From my room I could literally see into Karen Berger's corner office. To this day I'm still not sure if this was a deliberate plan to keep an eye on me. On the evening of my first day I wandered out of the hotel turned left and started strolling. I felt like I was in a movie. Everything felt so strangely familiar, as I'd seen these streets a million times in films and TV shows. The vast skyscrapers caused a crick in my neck as I strained to watch them disappear into the low-lying cloud cover. The yellow cabs cruised by, like old friends I'd never met. The "Walk" "Don't Walk" signs flashed at me in an overly familiar manner. It felt like home.

Beaming, I strolled down 7th Avenue, fairly confident of my destination. Then doubt started to creep in and I decided to confirm my directional beliefs. A woman was walking towards me, and when she was in earshot I said, "Excuse me." She leapt four foot in the air and looked terrified that I was about to mug her (or possibly, with my overly friendly grin, induct her into Scientology). "Am I heading the right way for Times Square?" She nodded and hurried on, giving me as wide a berth as possible. To be fair, these were the days before Mayor Giuliani kicked ass and gentrified the whole of Manhattan and the island was a lot edgier back then (in a bad way). But to a young, good-looking, naïve English boy it was one big adventure. It's a wonder I wasn't held at gunpoint, stripped naked and molested in some dark alleyway.

On the first day in the DC office I waited in reception for Karen to come down. On the wall was a life-size statue of Superman smashing through the wall, flying. Real bricks were exposed and behind was a painted scene of Metropolis, complete with the Daily Planet building in the background.

The DC offices were split on two floors, which meant a lot of up and down stairs through a convoluted security system. I was given the guided tour. We started in Karen's impressive office and she took me to meet the short, bespectled, moustachioed Paul Levitz, Executive VP & Publisher. He, in turn, took me into see the head honcho, the "Queen of Comics" The President of DC, Jenette Khan. Jenette had joined DC 17 years previously as Publisher and had risen to the top like so much cream. Her dress sense was legendary and she didn't disappoint, greeting me in a black-sequined top and an ill-advised above-the-knee skirt. I confess I was absolutely terrified, but her warm welcome and broad smile alleviated any fears.

Jenette's office was an incredible homage to pop art and pop culture. There were glass cabinets filled with action figures and unusual ornaments. Her desk was a modernist work of art, a black irregular shape with red and yellow edging. She was, and still is, a huge supporter and collector of modern art and sculpture, hardly surprising seeing as she graduated from Harvard University with honors in art history, specializing in 20th-century art, and later held a fellowship at the Museum of Modern Art.

But the thing I'll always remember about her office was the carpet. The carpet was yellow. I mean *really* yellow. So yellow that when I close my eyes right now I can still see it seared on to my retinas. To paraphrase Spinal Tap's Nigel Tufnel, "It's like, how much more yellow could this be? And the answer is none. None more yellow."

Finally, I was introduced to my US equivalents, fellow assistant Vertigo editors Shelly Roeberg (later Shelly Bond) and Julie Rottenberg. At points it felt like I was the only gentile at Vertigo. Julie was short with red hair and stylish glasses and a warm personality. She was Stuart Moore's Assistant. When she eventually left Vertigo she managed to get a job as a scriptwriter, editor, and finally producer working on a TV series called *Sex in the City*, where she was nominated for several Emmys.

Shelly was also short and had jet black hair and thick scarlet lipstick and was Karen's assistant. We'd all started at Vertigo at approximately the same time. Both of them shared a tiny windowless office and computer, and they had to squeeze me in for a week.

That week whizzed by in a blur of intense information downloads on the working systems of DC, meeting the production teams, Terri Cunningham in the legal department, mixed with a whirl of social engagements: Chinese lunch with Stuart, Julie, and then-*Black Orchid* artist Rebecca Guay; lunch with Production Manager and colourist Rick Taylor; Thursday night drinks in a local bar with the sales and marketing team of Bob Wayne, Patty Jeres and Vince Letterio, Superman Group Editor Mike Carlin, and numerous other DC crew. Before I knew it, it was Friday.

At that point Lou Stathis had not been with Vertigo long and as its newest editor, replacing Tom Peyer, he kindly took me under his wing and agreed to show this wide-eyed Brit New York proper on Saturday afternoon. He and his then-girlfriend met me at the hotel and we took the subway downtown. They took me all around Chinatown and we ended up in a spit'n'sawdust bar in Little Italy. I looked on the wall and there were photos of the barman with great Italian Americans like Madonna and Sinatra. As we were having a beer, this goomba walked in wearing a suit jacket over a black polo neck with a gold crucifix necklace. He walked over to the juke-box and chucked in a couple of quarters. Horns blasted out, "Pab Pab Ba-Da-Pab, Pab Pab Ba-Da-Pab, Pab Pab Ba-Da-Pab, Pab." And then

"Old Blue Eyes" opened his mouth, "Start spreading the news…" This was it, I thought, I've stumbled into a living cliché. This is where they take tourists to experience Italian Americans in fancy dress putting Frank Sinatra on singing *New York, New York*. I was in SopranosWorld™. I half expected the barman to turn out to be an animatronic, spouting homilies like "'Ey 'ow ya doin'?" "Bada-Bing, Bada-Boom!" But it was all very surreally real.

Four years later Lou would be dead, killed by a brain tumour. His story was partly fictionalised in Paul Jenkins and Paul Pope's deeply moving *Hellblazer* story, *Tell Me*, which appeared in the 1998 *Vertigo Winter's Edge* #1 anthology. I never forgot Lou's kindness that day, taking time out of his precious weekend to show me around.

I spent my last day doing the touristy things like visiting the Metropolitan Museum of Art, Central Park, and Liberty Island where I climbed the Statue (scene of the climax of the 2000 movie, *X-Men*). I thought about going up to the Windows on the World restaurant at the top of the World Trade Centre, but decided against it. I have a policy of always leaving at least one thing to do when I visit a new city. That way I have something to come back for. I'd get to the top of the Twin Towers when I return, I figured. How wrong could I be? By the time I eventually made it back to New York the Towers no longer existed.

When I returned to London it was with a sense of being part of a larger community that was more than just Art and I. It was a great feeling. I truly felt like I was part of the DC family.

The next month it was time for UKCAC again. These were the glory daze. DC were seriously courting British talent and sent over no less than nine editors and staff that year, including Karen, Bob Wayne, Patty Jeres, Dan Raspler, Andy Helfer, Lou Stathis and my

Stateside contemporary Shelly Roeberg. In contrast, these days, on average, just one or two editors make it over to the UK a year.

As the host office, it was up to Art and I to arrange the DC party on the Friday night. This was an annual event as a way of saying thank you to all the freelancers for the hard work they'd done over the past 12 months. Art picked the gay-friendly café/bar, The Edge, on Soho Square as the venue—primarily because he loved their sundried tomatoes on ciabatta.

Being a select affair, there was much discussion about who did and didn't get in. Technically, it should've been strictly freelancers (plus partners) who'd worked for DC over the last year, plus the odd guest who we were trying to win over. In reality there were a considerable amount of non-DC artists, and even non-comics bods on Art's final guest list (including the Warner Brothers gang). Consequently, both floors of the bar were crammed with heaving bodies all desperate to drain the venue dry before the free bar ran out.

With a few exceptions, comic creators aren't generally the most chic group of people, but usually the collection of writers, artists, colourists and letterers made a bit of an effort and dressed up for the party. After all, this was a chance to press the flesh with editors and to thank the hand that, quite literally that night, fed them. Art, in his ever-understated way, arrived late in black tie, blowing everyone's efforts out the water. As Mark Millar recalled "Art Young looked particularly dashing in his dinner suit, lending a touch of elegance and class to an otherwise sartorially bankrupt convention."

Once all the food and drink had been consumed, everyone decamped back to the Bloomsbury Crest Hotel bar, the central hub of late night drinking sessions for many years.

Comic conventions invariably are split into four basic activities; rummaging around dealer's halls, hoping to pick up a bargain comic or graphic novel; visiting panel sessions where writers and artists talk about their latest works; joining vast queues in the vain hope of getting a sketch or a comic signed; and drinking heavily in the bar. Needless to say the latter was the most popular activity with the professionals.

After everyone had returned from the various publisher-paid parties and meals, they would all congregate at the hotel bar and continue imbibing until dawn. Things could get pretty chaotic and often the bar staff would close the bar in a vague hope to dissuade the non-residents, and to encourage the residents to go to bed. It never worked. More often than not Steve Dillon and Garth Ennis led the Charge of the Light Ale Brigade, passing a couple of pint glasses around and getting everyone to chuck in a quid or two in order to bribe the staff to keep the bar open. It worked every time.

The following day, feeling distinctly lacklustre, I "hosted" a "*2000 AD* Love-in" with Grant, Garth, Mark Millar—the self-professed "Poor man's Grant Morrison"—and others. In typically flamboyant style—rather than having a normal prosaic panel discussion, with everyone sitting at a table on stage and answering questions from the audience—Grant and Mark scattered bean bags over the stage and invited the entire audience to come up and join them in a mass lounge. Champagne bottles were uncorked and passed round, along with assorted M&Ms. Halfway through the panel the booze ran out so Grant grabbed a volunteer from the audience, gave him £200 and told him to get some more. Amazingly, the bloke returned with several bottles a few minutes later, to much cheering. As Mark typically exaggerated later, "Fifty bottles of champagne, three quid's worth of bananas and one hour with comics gurus, Millar and Morrison. It could have been the best day of your life." In fact, there was only two quid's worth of bananas.

Shelly stayed in the UK after UKCAC. It was no secret that she coveted Art's exulted position, and as a fellow Anglophile (and Paul Weller obsessive) she was keen to work with as many Brits as possible, particularly Milligan, and was constantly trying to romance creators away from us. The following weekend after the convention Shelly and I made the now familiar trek down to see the Worthing gang. It was a bitter winter, and neither of us had packed appropriately. I can't recall whether we'd even intended to stay down overnight, or simply that we just missed the last train back to London, but after the obligatory night out at The Factory with Philip and Glyn we were given the keys to Hewlett's house to crash in. Jamie and Alan were in L.A. discussing the forthcoming *Tank Girl* movie. The house was freezing, and—after discovering a Polaroid of Jamie with Adam Ant in the very kitchen we were standing in (I guess Mr. Ant had used the phone number I'd given him in Comic Showcase, all those years ago)—we completely failed to discover how to turn the central heating on. Thus, Shelly and I were reduced to huddling around a two bar electric fire in the living room and trying to sleep on a hard chair and sofa, respectively, fully clothed, sans blankets. It was one of the most miserable nights of my life. I thought back to that uncomfortable night at my first UKCAC in the cold hall and realised how little my life had actually moved on.

Jamie and Alan eventually returned from L.A. with lots of anecdotes about how they were schmoozed by Hollywood. They'd gone over with Tom Astor, *Deadline*'s publisher, to meet with various lawyers and producers. There they were, standing on a wet, cold Worthing train platform and 24 hours later were being driven around La La Land in an open top sports car with a producer giving them spiel:

"You know, guys, making a movie is like making a pizza."

Jamie and Alan stared at the schmoozer incredulously.

"It takes lots of different levels."

"You're just talking bollocks aint yer, mate?" Jamie sneered.

"Oh God," thought Tom, "they've just screwed the deal."

The producer eyed Jamie with suspicion, then smiled.

"You know, I love your English sense of humour."

That Christmas all the editors were given an exclusive (there were only eight made) Vertigo watch which had a black leather strap, gold edging and hands, and the swirly Vertigo logo in purple on the face. It looked initially impressive but—despite me never wearing it—subsequently broke after six months.

Returning from the Christmas break, we decided that we needed a jolly in France and headed back to Angoulême in January, 1994. Ostensibly, this was a "fact finding mission" but I don't recall doing a jot of work. The whole Les Cartoonistes Dangereux gang were there along with Art, Paul, Ellie, and DC Comics' International Rights Manager, Francine Burke (who was the only one actually grafting).

By March the whole *Tank Girl* movie publicity behemoth was rolling at full pelt and it seemed to be slightly overwhelming Jamie and Alan somewhat. The newspapers had announced that the producers of the film were going to be holding open auditions for the titular role at the MGM Trocadero cinema, Piccadilly, in the West End of London.

The ad in *The Stage* read: "...A stunning woman in her twenties—Spirited, sexy, quick-witted, irreverent and tough, possessing a rugged rock and roll spirit! Able to take care of herself in most situations, both physically and mentally, and rides a water buffalo..." That pretty much summed up TG's personality well, except they missed out the bit about snogging kangaroos.

Around 11am Peter Milligan, Glyn Dillon, Art and I strolled down from the Vertigo office to check out all the hoo-ha. Outside the cinema was a vast line of hundreds and hundreds of aspiring actresses. There was everything from punk girls, riot grrls, ginger girls, scary girls, sporty girls, posh girls, and cute girls. Some were completely dressed in Tank Girl costumes, with shaved head and baseball bat, while most were dressed more prosaically. Some were obviously straight out of Italia Conti whilst others look like they'd just wondered past and joined the queue for something to do. However, nearly all of them had attitude in spades. Just like their hero, Tank Girl, these girls were not to be fucked with. This was "girl power" before the term had even been invented, packaged and commodified.

Inside the cinema we met Rachel Talalay, the director, and sat down towards the back with Jamie and Alan. What happened next was a cross between a visit to Bedlam and some perverse distortion of a Miss World contest. The vast line-up of girls were invited into the cinema, five at a time. Some were asked to tell the director and producers about themselves, while others were asked to read one line from the script and then thanked for their time. This was lip service at best. One particularly outraged hopeful, understandably pissed off with this brief "audition," shouted out to the back, "Which one of you's Jamie Hewlett?" Jamie judiciously slid lower into his chair. "You're fuckin' with people's lives!!" After an endless succession of various vacuous attempts to engage the producers and Rachel, the list of hopefuls tended to blend into one after a while. There were a few who stood out, including a punk girl who angle-ground a steel codpiece, causing sparks to fly.

Next, a girl—sensing she had nothing to lose (apart from possibly her dignity)—whipped her top off to flash her impressive breasts at us. I turned to Glyn who smiled, gave me a thumbs-up and mouthed "Cheer!"

After the bare-breasted lady there was smartly dressed 19-year-old girl, with long brown hair and large silver hoop earrings and a grey suit, called Victoria Addams-Wood who said, "I don't look at all right for this part, but I'm an actress!" She looked like a secretary who'd just stepped out of the office on her lunch break. We didn't pay her much attention. Then some red-head girl and dressed in a pink crop top said "Hi, My name's Geri, like Tom and Jerry, but spelt differently, I'm a jack of all trades, got a quirky sense of humour... I'm twenty-two and a Leo. I'm loud and I'm proud and I think I'd make a great Tank Girl." She was as remarkable as Victoria. Neither of them got the role. Apparently, they went on to form a girl band called the Spice Girls. You may have heard of them.

The whole Tank Girl audition was, of course, a sham and a huge publicity stunt. They already knew who was going to be cast, and it wasn't going to be some completely untested stranger off the street. There was too much of MGM's money at stake for that (supposedly $25 million's worth). The vastly over-rated, and irritatingly squeaky voiced, Lori Petty had already been chosen for the role, much to many hopefuls' anger.

That anger spilled over to the cinema-goers and TG fans when the film came out. The Studio couldn't help fiddling with the film. MGM insisted on cutting a scene of Tank Girl and her kangaroo boyfriend Booga reclining after sex, despite allegedly spending $5,000 on a prosthetic penis for Booga. All this dicking around meant the very thing that made Tank Girl Tank Girl—the sex, swearing and utter disrespect for everything—had been erased from the film. Typically, Hollywood didn't "get it". The same thing happened with Sylvester

Stallone's *Judge Dredd*, also released that year, with Sly breaking the golden rule, by removing the "lawman of the future's" helmet.

Aware of the huge Tank Girl backlash the film unleashed, Alan and Jamie took the money and ran. Alan became a publican in Berwick-Upon-Tweed and Jamie cut all ties with his comic friends, shacked up with Damon Albarn and developed an equestrian habit for a few years, before the duo resurfaced as the mythical pop band, Gorillaz.

Returning to the Vertigo office I got stuck into the first original graphic novel I'd worked on, *The Mystery Play* written by Morrison and exquisitely painted by Jon J. Muth. J's pages were enormous thick black boards with individual, sublime watercolors glued on and arranged as panels. As is so often the way, the printed version doesn't do the artwork one tenth of the justice it deserves. "The story is set in the real world," Morrison revealed in an interview in *Hero Illustrated* #9 (March, 1994), "but it has a lot of strange hallucinatory interludes. That works well if you get a painter like Jon who's perfect at capturing all these details of the real world. I think that really worked well in the story, because when it goes into the hallucinatory stuff, you can't tell the difference, and it hopefully messes up the reader's perception of what's real and what's not."

Throughout the process, looking at the script and the artwork, I began to see deeper meanings, secret messages, and hidden sub-texts throughout. When I asked Grant whether they were intentional "Easter eggs" hidden for the reader to decode, his response was a blithe and enigmatic, "Aye, if you like." I never discovered whether these were deliberate interconnections or some kind of weird meta-evolutionary text that could be read in a million different ways by each reader—everyone seeing the patterns they wanted to see in some sequential art simulacra. It still stands as one of Grant's most underrated works, and I'd recommend reading it.

Before we knew it, it was time to head back up north again for GlasCAC 94. Returning to the Copthorne hotel, Friday night was spent drinking with the crew as per usual. I asked Will Simpson to do me a sketch and expected a brief, but competent, ten-minute doodle. What I got was an hour-long stunning work of art. It was one of the *Vamps* (the series he was drawing for Vertigo at the time, written by Elaine Lee) in exquisite pencil. I plied him with many pints as a thank you. As the night wore on, and the crowds began to thin out we were reduced to a small hardcore including Steve Dillon. Dillon had a reputation for always being the last to bed, and one that had remained unchallenged for years. In fact you'd very rarely find him at any convention during the day, as—like some alcoholic vampire—he would only emerge as the sun set, to drain the Guinness from the bar—the stout is the life!—before disappearing as day broke.

But here we were, and the sun was up. The hotel staff were laying out the tables for breakfast when all of a sudden, at about 7am, Dillon stood up and announced, "Right. I'm off to bed." I'd done it! After four years of trying, I'd stayed up later than Dillon! It was my proudest moment of any convention. Too bad there were so few people left sober/conscious/alive to witness it. But, of course, the consequences of such foolishness plagued me for the rest of the day; shakes, cold sweats and sheer exhaustion. It felt as if most conventions were spent on an alcoholic rollercoaster, evenings of high intoxication followed by days of rueful tremors. I was, by no means, the worst offender, and in fact downing vast quantities of booze has always been seen as a mark of a man in the British comic industry. That attitude has unfortunately led to the physical ruination of a number of comic professionals. And, as I was soon to find out, me.

As the summer hoved into view I took the offer of a trip to visit my friend Garth Ennis in Belfast. That was my first in a litany of ill-conceived judgements. I'd never been to Northern Ireland before, and it was during the "Troubles". It was with the decades-long conflict between Protestants and Catholics, Nationalists and Republicans that Garth made his name in the serialised *Troubled Souls* in *Crisis*. It took some time getting used to seeing soldiers armed to the teeth and roaming the streets of Belfast, and green British Army Range Rovers zooming about the city. But pretty soon I was ignoring these teen-soldiers just like the locals. It's incredible how quickly one becomes acclimatised to living in a war zone.

That week was a haze of incessant drinking and eating. Most evenings started with a takeaway and a film accompanied by a nice red from Garth's extensive wine "cellar." Then it was down to the Crown (Belfast's oldest pub and guest-location in more than a few Ennis comics) for a few pints.

One night, a huge group of us (including Will Simpson) went to Paul Rankin's Michelin-starred Roscoff Restaurant, enjoying Cognac and cigars and benefiting from Garth's gregarious nature.

Then, in order to save my liver, or so I thought, I headed up to stay with Will and his family for a few days in Glenarm, a small fishing village north of Belfast. However, the alcohol followed and flowed. We went to the local pub, which was little more than a house with a dirt floor and a makeshift bar, known as the "Stump and Thresher" on account of so many limbs missing from the locals. The pub was immortalised in Ennis and John McCrea's *Dicks*.

On reaching Belfast for the last couple of days, the whirlwind of late night drinking intensified, until the morning of my departure. On awaking, with barely four hours until my flight home, I crawled to Ennis' bathroom, lay on the floor, clinging onto the toilet. "You've poisoned me," I moaned. "You bastar-blueghhhh" as I emptied what little contents of my stomach remained. Eventually I drew myself up shakily, dressed and managed to hold it together enough to make it back to England. I learnt a very valuable lesson that night— never to try and out-drink an Irishman. Unfortunately it's a lesson I frequently forget.

The summer drifted by in a haze of Ecstasy-laden parties held at Paul and Elllie's. There was a hardcore gang that included Marvel UK writer Simon Jowett and his fiancée Annabel, Big A, Peter Milligan and his partner, Carol, Ilya, and many others. Those crazy Friday and Saturday nights were balanced by washed-out Sunday afternoons that merged into evenings with Hal Hartley movies and the incredibly camp *Kids in the Hall*—with its creepy chicken lady, "Gotta get laid. Gotta get laid" and crazy man, "I'm crushing your head"—taking the edge off those hard comedowns.

On one particularly decadent bash in the basement where I was first introduced to "Doves", the "brand name" of our favourite MDMA pills, I peaked and troughed throughout the night. Little things—like moving my head too fast—kicked off another rush of euphoria, as I chain-smoked all my Marlboro Lights. When I'd smoked all I could smoke, and could smoke no more, I moved onto Art's Menthol cigarettes. They were like a breath of fresh air. It was as if I'd set fire to one end of a pack of Polo mints and was puffing away merrily on them. I could've smoked all night. And I did. They say that marijuana is a gateway drug. It's true. It leads on to a life-long nicotine addiction that's near-impossible to kick.

I passed out back at Art's flat. I woke up on the sofa, feeling as if a pig had shat in my head, and I'd apparently eaten the contents of Art's ashtray. I staggered to the dark, forbidding olive-green bathroom and ran the tap in the desperate hope for water that resembled something other than lukewarm from either tap, and failed. I splashed my face, swilled my mouth with some of Art's toothpaste and staggered out the door. As I left I heard Art murmur from the bedroom, "I'll be there shortly. Start without me." I managed to make it down the lift, and zigzagged along Broadwick Street to the office, still semi-intoxicated. It took a whole 10 minutes instead of the usual four. I grunted as pleasantly as I could to the security guard and staggered into the lift to the top floor. Finally, after heroically making a cup of tea, I sat down at my desk at 11am and stared at the wall for two hours. The phone rang. "Hey, it's me," said the withered American voice. "I'm not feeling so good, so I don't think I'll be in today. Call me if anything happens."

The following week Alan Moore was giving a reading in a small basement bar just off Tottenham Court Road, so Brad Brooks and I popped down. I seem to recall it was for his forthcoming novel, *Voice of the Fire*. At the time, to my untrained philistine ear, it seemed desperately convoluted and pretentious, but I've always loved his work so struggled on with it, listening attentively.

I hadn't seen Alan since UKCAC '87 and thought it would be good to say hello afterwards, as a representative of DC Comics. In my blissfully naive (and slightly inebriated) state I was completely unaware of the fractures that were appearing in Alan's relationship with DC over the *Watchmen* rights, and sauntered up to him jovially and started chatting. He was as pleasant and convivial as he'd been previously (and as he has been in every single encounter since) but as soon as I let slip that I was working for Vertigo UK something changed. His face dropped and became a mix of rage and disgust, as if I'd just told him I'd pissed in his pint. He turned around and stormed off, leaving me completely baffled as to what I'd said wrong. With hindsight, I suspect he thought I'd been put up to this by DC to try and soft soap him. But this genuinely wasn't the case and the whole incident left me a tad shaken. I left in a daze, a little distraught that I'd apparently enraged one of my favourite writers.

When I think back to those days my hedonism knew no bounds, both chemically and sexually. I was like a rutting bull on heat who's swallowed a fistful of Viagra washed down with Spanish Fly. In the space of 18 months I'd brutally and heartlessly dropped my long-term girlfriend of four years; slept with three women at Warner's and two men (not at Warner's), had a threesome with two lovely women, and managed a brief, but passionate affair with a beautiful Welsh Goddess, who I'd met at one of Glenn & Nikki Fabry's legendary Christmas parties. Not to mention the numerous fumbled, ecstasy-induced attempts at "seduction" with other co-workers, "We should all just sleep together! We should just have sex! That's what we should do! Right now! Let's have sex! Now! That'd be great! Right? Right?" That was the *real* downside of Methylenedioxymethamphetamine. Not the washed-out, wasted, achy Sundays. Not the mid-week blues comedown. It was the fact that it forced you to spout complete and utter bollocks incessantly. My brain was constantly slipping out of gear before I opened my gob at the best of times, but Ecstasy made it run off like a diarrhoeic Mo Farah. Couple that with a complete lack of social inhibition and self-control and it was a recipe for disaster.

The UK office had always railed against doing any long ongoing series, for fear of losing direction and readership, and Art getting bored—and our titles were always very writer-led—so it seemed natural for us to launch our own imprint-within-an-imprint with the Vertigo Voices range. These were a series of four one-shot stories, each with a distinct writer's voice. Or as we put in the house ad, "Our most outspoken writers are about to sound off"—we wrote and designed all the in-house adverts for our titles.

Not quite full books, but twice the length of a standard 24-page comic, these were "graphic novellas." There was *Face* by Milligan and Fegredo, "from the team that brought you *Enigma*." This was a tense thriller set around the themes of "The nature of art. The nature of beauty. The nature of horror," and plastic surgery, a good decade before *Nip/Tuck* hit the small screen. It's still one of my favourite comics and one of the ones I'm most proud to have worked on. There's been talk of turning it into a film for years, but having seen the amateurish trailer that was made, I don't stand much hope for it making the big screen any time soon. If anyone was to direct it, David Cronenberg would be the perfect choice.

Face, a glitzy/grisly L.A.-set suspense was accompanied by Jamie Delano and Al Davison's grim British kitchen sink drama, *Tainted*. This originally started out as *Dead Man's Shoes*, a story of a man who inadvertently kills another and then assumes his identity and life. The finished script was brilliant. Unfortunately a friend of Jamie's pointed out that there was already a book of the same name, with a similar story (written by H.C. Bailey in 1942). Neither he, Art, nor I had heard of it, let alone read it. It was just one of those strange "coincidences"—an idea washed up from Jung's collective unconscious. Rather than risk being accused of plagiarism Jamie, extremely professionally, scrapped the entire script and started again. The end result was *Tainted*. This was a dark, depressing tale of a lonely man, with repressed secrets, who rents rooms in his house to a drug-addict and a nurse with issues of her own. It read like *EastEnders* on Mogadons. In direct contrast, Grant Morrison and Philip Bond's gleefully bright and bouncy, anarchic and hedonistic *Kill Your Boyfriend* took the lovers-on-the-run-from-the-police tropes from US literature and mythos, and transposed them into Middle England, creating an absurd attack on mundane modernity. Little wonder that this was the only title of the three to be reprinted.

It was also, "the glory days of *Bizarre Boys*—the lost Milligan/Morrison/Hewlett project," Grant recalled in an interview. *Bizarre Boys* was intended as the fourth title in the Voices quartet. The idea was for it to be written in one day, simultaneously by Pete and Grant under the pseudonyms of Millison and Morrigan. The story would take place on that same day and culminate in a Bizarre Boys day, mirroring James Joyce's Bloomsday from *Ulysses*. Only, it never happened. According to the sales blurb we wrote, it was supposed to be "a story within a story within a story. It's about some fictional characters called the Bizarre Boys, and about the writers who write them, and about the writers who are writing about the writers… There are two voices telling the tale of *Bizarre Boys*, and they don't agree with each other at all. *Bizarre Boys* is a comic about a comic and about the process of putting together a comic. It's a sparkling tapestry of post-modernism and a fast-moving breathless chase across time and space." Unfortunately, the reality was a mess. Jamie was too busy with the *Tank Girl* movie and only ever produced a couple of drawings. Pete went up to Glasgow to visit Grant, but as the Scotsman confessed a decade later, things didn't go well. "…Pete traveled 400 miles to Glasgow for a dynamic, outrageous, drug-fueled plotting session. This was to be Bizarre Boys Day—the strangest, most deranged 24 hours of our lives. Instead we spent the entire day and night zoned out in front of afternoon, then evening, then nighttime television, unable to produce a single interesting thought between us." I guess any project that—despite its grandiose, literary aspirations—is named after a gay porn mag had the dice loaded against it from the start.

Almost a year after the previous titles, the fourth, and final, title in the Vertigo Voices experiment eventually took the form of Milligan's cannibal comedy, *The Eaters*, expertly illustrated by Yorkshire softman, Dean Ormston.

In September, Art was called back for a few meetings with Karen at DC's New York offices for a couple of weeks. While he was away, he asked me to look after his cat, Max, who had just been released from six month's captivity in quarantine (Art visited him once a week).

I opened the door of Art's flat and the familiar reek of cat shit and piss assaulted my nostrils. Max was a house, or rather, a flat cat. That is, he never went outdoors. Basically, because there wasn't an outdoors to go out to. Art's abode was on the 9th floor of an exclusive tower block on the edge of Carnaby Street right in the heart of the West End. His neighbours were all from the great and good, nouveau riche and old money, designers and creatives of all sorts, including the cartoonist Gray Jolliffe (creator of *Wicked Willie*).

But what it made up for in location and neighbours it lacked in space and fresh air. As Max was in the flat 24/7 the windows could never be fully opened, and the heating seemed to be uncontrollably and permanently set on 120 degrees Celsius. This, combined with the contents of Max's litter tray, created a malodorous, near toxic, atmosphere that took at least quarter of an hour to acclimatise to.

It was Cheeky's birthday, so I suggested that we (and the Les Cartoonistes… crowd) have a few drinks in town, and then have a party and crash at Art's, rather than having to schlep our various ways home across London.

After frequenting numerous Soho drinking holes, we eventually we staggered back to my boss' apartment (as he called it) and carried on drinking heavily. At some point in the proceedings someone decided to try and pick up Max. For an overweight cat he could move surprisingly fast when he wanted to and he was in no mood to be man handled by a bunch of drunken idiots. Things became hazy and I awoke dehydrated, drooling into a pillow, semi-clothed. I staggered into the living room where various carcasses had been draped over the sofa, chairs and floor. I nudged one of the corpses, which stirred.

"Have you seen Max?" I asked, as the kettle boiled in the micro-kitchen.

"What?" Replied the cadaver.

"Max. The cat."

"Uh, no."

I figured he was hiding in a cupboard, or under the bed after the unnecessary trauma we'd put him through the previous night. Once all the bodies had been reanimated through tea and coffee our search for the terrorised tabby began in earnest. Remembering that Art's flat consisted of a bathroom, a kitchen, a bedroom and a living room, each about the size of a Luton van, the search didn't take very long. Max was nowhere to be seen. We sat down with more tea and tried to recall last night's events.

"Perhaps he got out the front door?" Someone suggested. I opened it and looked down the hall. Nothing. Hoping against hope I walked through the fire doors to the lift. Still nothing. It'd be a miracle if he'd got through the security locked door and into the lift, but I took it down to the lobby just in case.

I returned empty handed with mounting dread in my stomach. I sat down in the living room to plan the next course of action. Then I saw it.

"How long's that fucking window been open?!" I squeaked, in the high pitch tone I reserve for when very stressed.

"I dunno."

"Shit. Fuck. The only thing Art asked me to do was look after the cat and now it's jumped out the fucking window." I was distraught.

"FUCK!" I added for emphasis. That was it, my job was over. There was no way I could get out of this. I leaned out the window and looked at the 80 foot drop below, trying to make out a feline carcass lying on the ground.

"Perhaps it landed on its feet?" Someone added for cold comfort.

"Yeah, and then its feet were pile-driven up through its shoulder blades." I snapped. I felt dizzy and sick and sat down at the dining table. How the hell was I going to explain this? I couldn't think.

"Look!" Cheeky said pointing at the window.

"Shit!" I replied.

"Maow," said Max.

He was perched precariously on the three-inch wide ledge outside.

"Quick, everyone back away slowly from the window. For fuck's sake don't do anything to startle him."

The next 10 minutes were hell, as the bastard cat hung around outside taunting us, as if doing a high-wire act. One false slip and it was all over for him and me. Eventually he walked up to the window, hopped in and blithely went to his food bowl as if to say, "That'll teach you fuckers to fuck around with me."

I slammed the window shut and shook with shock for a few minutes. Art never found out how close his beloved Max came to being street pizza. I was never really a "cat person" but after that I developed a serious allergy to them.

Without warning it was October and UKCAC again. Time was rushing past faster than Ayrton Senna on amphetamines. Friday night of the convention saw Art and I hosting the official DC party once more. After the cramped quarters of The Edge the previous year, we decided to upscale the affair and booked out the entire first floor of the swanky restaurant, Soho Soho. Always bigger, always better. There were the usual coterie of hangers on and blaggers who had nothing to do with DC Comics, that I'd managed to smuggle in, including most of Les Cartoonistes, my then-girlfriend, the Welsh Goddess, and Michael Bennent, the Teutonic editor of *Crisis*. Michael was a relative of Johnny Weissmuller—the Olympic swimmer and the best Tarzan, in my opinion—and was spending far too much time hanging round my girlfriend for my liking. Fellow LCD co-founders, Brad and Faz, were bizarrely discussing beachwear with Bennent.

"So, you're telling me you don't have any shorts?" Brad asked, incredulously.

"I have some… but they are leather," came the Germanic reply.

"Lederhosen? You're talking about lederhosen!"

Bennent looked into his champagne glass shamefully, as if confessing to buggering a goat.

"Yes, I have lederhosen."

Fucker still ran off with my girlfriend.

We ran the Vertigo Panel on Saturday at 2pm and the convention booklet described it as, "Large numbers of Vertigo creators and editorial staff will be planted among you. You'll be learning more about them and their influences as they learn more about you and your life." What the fuck were we on about? To be brutally honest

I can't remember a thing about that panel. If I was there I must've been drunk.

Most of my days at conventions were spent doing portfolio reviews. This was an arduous way of spotting new talent. Long before the internet the only real access writers and artists had to editors was at the conventions, so we'd all spend a good few hours going through artists' work. Occasionally you'd find a really exceptional artist who you could snap up before anyone discovered them. You'd also find the occasional loon, who'd drawn stick figures in green biro and expected to be given their own 12-issue Superman miniseries. But more often than not you'd just see an endless queue of average, mediocre artists, some with talent still in its pupa stage, ready to blossom in a couple of years, and some who should have never been given access to art materials in the first place.

The hardest thing was looking at ways in which you could provide constructive criticism without destroying their dreams. We'd offer advice on anatomy, perspective, ways to keep a panel interesting, leaving "dead space" for lettering, etc. For a bunch of artists who wanted to work in comics, there were a surprising amount who had little idea of what storytelling or page composition were. One of those rare occasions, when I knew all hope was lost—but I didn't want to stamp all over their fragile souls—I'd find myself struggling to say something positive about the art, "So, you drew this in pencil, did you?" was all I could muster, as I stared into their glassy, puppy dog eyes. Shooting them in the face would've been kinder. At least it would've been quicker than the death of a thousand rejection letters.

It was as brutal an experience as crossing the *Dragon's Den* with *The Apprentice* and a touch of *X-Factor* thrown in. But it was also the way that many comic artists got their first break. However, after three hours of staring at badly drawn pictures of Batman, you do start to lose the will to live.

That night we took a select horde of creators over to Lee Ho Fook's, the best Chinese restaurant in London, immortalised in Warren Zevon's *Werewolves of London*, and gorged ourselves over dim sum, beef chow mein and copious Singha beers. Then it was back to the Bloomsbury Crest for more beers and shouting in the bar.

I was no stranger to the odd bit of puff. Like most teenage boys, I'd had the occasional toke on a joint since I was 15, but had not really dabbled in the murky waters of hallucinogenics. All that changed at 1994's UK Comic Art Convention.

Two famous comic creators, let's call them G and J, to protect their anonymity, decided to take me under their wings and introduce me to this fun guy, fungi. Recreational drugs are "meat and 'taters" to the creative community. I defy anyone to point out a great work of art that wasn't inspired by some kind of altered state, be it booze, drugs or insanity. Or preferably, all three. Admittedly UKCAC was perhaps not the most conducive setting for one's first journey into the mind on psilocybin. I was breaking at least one of Timothy Leary's "set and setting" rules, if not both of them.

Regardless, we ascended to G's hotel room where he brewed up a bitter black tea made from the dried mushrooms. We swallowed the acrid liquid and waited. And waited. And waited. Eventually J suggested that we take a walk in the tradition of Guy Debord and the Parisian Letterists who'd wander the city in a state of "dérive" experiencing and rediscovering the urban landscape in new ways.

We took the lift down, judiciously avoiding the bar, and stepped out into the night. It was unseasonably warm and at first everything was fine. All the streetlights twinkled as if shot through a starlight filter.

Then waves of paranoia began to wash over me. Every car was a cop car. And they could tell, just by looking, that I was off my tits. I was going to be stitched up like a kipper by the rozzers for sure.

Yet this paranoia was tempered with the unerring fact that I knew every single person on the street. All my friends were out and about walking up and down just like we were. I cheerily walked up to Alan Martin with a smile and an extended hand, only to be greeted by a complete stranger. Where had Alan gone? My mind was doing a Derren Brown number on me. It began spitting a light rain.

Then I saw an actual *real* police car and my paranoia went into overdrive. I suppressed my instinctual flight or fight impulse. Perhaps they'd think I was drunk. Yeah, that's it, drunk. The socially acceptable way to wander the streets of a large metropolis on a Saturday night with an utter absence of faculties. The police car passed, blissfully oblivious to my panic. As the three of us amiably ambled the streets of London we suddenly realised that we were somehow, subconsciously taking the same path that William Gull instructs his coachman, Nettley, to follow in Alan Moore and Eddie Campbell's *From Hell*, being serialised in *Taboo* at the time. Reaching Cleopatra's Needle on the bank of the Thames, slightly perturbed by the idea that Moore was manipulating our trip somehow, and finally succumbing to the increased precipitation, we made our way back towards the convention hotel. G and J felt ready to face the drunken hordes of the hotel bar, but I was still far too off my face to contemplate any form of meaningful conversation, so retired to G's room for a bit.

I contently watched the radiator breathe in and out. Slowly and rhythmically expanding and contracting. In. And. Out. Like a giant iron lung. I merrily conversed with the television announcer who very kindly wished me a goodnight and to look after myself, to which I replied it was a bit late to do that now.

Suddenly, my brothers-in-psychotropic-arms burst into the room admitting that they were in no way straight and facing an alcohol-fuelled bar full of comic creators, fanboys and assorted Brit Pop hanger-ons was not the thing to subject a fevered imagination to.

Stuart Moore popped up to the room and entertained us by reading a Biggles graphic novel out loud to us, with much hilarity. Which only serves to prove my point that watching people on drugs is incredibly boring if you're straight yourself.

Finally, about 2am, I felt straight enough to descend back down to the bar, where Art was sitting on the floor with a coterie around him. I tried to play things nonchalantly, but became hypnotised by the fact that it appeared that someone was turning the lights up and down as if on a dimmer switch. Yet no one else was remarking upon this so I remained silent but fascinated, and spent far too long staring at this visual mind-trick, so that undoubtedly everyone in the vicinity had noticed I was not entirely *compos mentis.*

After that, the rest of the night drifted past, but I emerged the other side pretty much unscathed—fatigued, but functional. The reality was that I'd crossed a Rubicon at that point. I'd got utterly fucked off my face in public and that had left me politically exposed.

I remember my first time out clubbing on E. Up until then I'd only every taken it round Paul and Ellie's, or someone else's house, listening to chilled ambient stuff like Orbital or Underworld's classic, *Dubnobasswithmyheadman* album. I still get goose pimples listening to the track, *Cowgirl.*

So around November/December 1994 "the deadbeat club" – about eight or nine of us, including Art, Paul, Big A, Ellie and others – decided to check out Club UK in Wandsworth, in South West London. It was at its peak and the legendary Final Frontier on a Friday night was running. All the big rave DJs played there, including Paul Oakenfold, Andrew Weatherall, Sven Vath and Moby. The place had a huge reputation as being a major centre for Ecstasy dealing.

It was a freezing night and after a few drinks out, we shared three cabs and got down there about midnight. We negotiated a massive queue, climbed, what seemed like, a thousand steps to get in, but stepping through the doors was like entering wonderland. Everything was already kicking off. The lightshows, lasers and people all annihilated my senses. And the heat was incredible. Everyone was stripping down to stay cool. The club was selling small bottles of "Club UK" water at £1.50, the same price as a vodka and orange. The club had been decorated with huge white inflatable stars and shapes.

We popped our pills before arriving and after the environment helped kick in the MDMA, I was off! Big smiles all round. Somehow we got split up and I found myself alone, wandering aimlessly looking for my mates. Everyone I saw was my best friend, until I got up close to them and realised that I didn't know them. It was UKCAC '94 all over again. Ecstasy breeds familiarity.

Then something happened. Maybe it was because I was in a big crowd on my own, feeling vulnerable, but something changed. The music started getting harder and faster, making my heartbeat increase. As the beats per minute started cranking up, the crowd suddenly changed from being lovely and friendly to dodgy and menacing. I was starting to freak out. I'd never had a bad time on E before and was starting to go into a major panic attack. I staggered into the chill out room to calm down. Bumping into Big A I crashed into a giant beanbag next to him. He started talking me out of it. After a while I started feeling better, so I decided to brave the dancefloor once more, but as soon as I got out there the bpm and fear gripped me again. Paul and Ellie realised I was freaking and decided to take me home.

Back in the taxi I was suddenly fine and all "Wha-hey, let's go back!" but my friends knew better and we went home and chilled. It was so wonderful they way they looked after me, my "surrogate parents"—I owe them a lot, as it could've gone "Pete Tong." Shortly after our excursion, there was a tragic death at Club UK and the police came down hard on the place with so many constant raids that it eventually had to shut down.

For those in the know, it was painfully obvious that so much of our output from the London office was heavily based on all our clubbing lifestyles. As Morrison reminisced in the back of 1998's re-release of *Kill Your Boyfriend*, "It makes me think of the soon-to-be-nostalgia 1990s and E and of reeling hysterical nights…" When it was our turn to produce Vertigo's special preview comic we naturally called it *Vertigo Rave*, with our mantra "Work all day, rave all night" as the tagline. We even had a cheesy sub-heading: "Bliss out at the Vertigo Rave" Most of this went over New York's head, but we were blatantly telling them what we were doing. We created rave-like flyers for distribution in the comic shops; "Lose yourself in the ambient feel." "This rave is a wicked sample of Vertigo's hottest new happenings." It all sounds desperately puerile and naïve now, in the cold light of an early misty morning, but we really believed in this shit back then.

But for every high, there has to be an equal and opposite low. And our highs were getting ever higher. We were reaching a tipping point beyond which there was nowhere to go but spiralling down…

CHAPTER FOUR
...WORRYING LOWS

"We didn't even get to try anal sex..."
"Maybe there's still time."

—**Kill Your Boyfriend**, Grant Morrison, Philip Bond & D'Israeli

O ne day in October 1993 we received a letter from a student. Nothing exceptional in that, except that it was from a female graduate with a Classics degree from University College of London who was very interested in comics, and Vertigo in particular. She was wondering if there was any chance of getting some work experience in our office (or an internship in Septic talk. Slave labour in plainspeak.) Her name was Helen and we thought it might be helpful to have an extra pair of hands to help us around the office, as we were being inundated by PR and marketing requests that were taking us away from editing books. And besides, it was a cheap way of expanding the UK empire. Little did I know, but that letter was to spell my doom.

We invited Helen in for an interview. She was a big girl. Tall and statuesque at 6' 1". Amazonian. She exuded strength that was offset by a physical gangliness and general clumsiness, which gave the appearance that she was still trying this body on for size. She sported short, chestnut brown hair, was nervously cheery (perhaps even more than me, which was unsettling) and greeted us with a big broad smile as she thrust out her large hand to shake. But beneath this apparent physical awkwardness and slightly goofy demeanour lay a very intelligent, razor sharp mind.

She seemed jovial enough, smart and enthusiastic, and both of us liked her, so we took her on. Best of all she was willing to learn the ropes for free. Helen literally lived about 10 doors down on Wardour Street, which was extremely convenient for all concerned.

She initially popped in for one or two days a week to help out and I was glad of the support.

At the weekends and evenings the Vertigo office was transformed into the secret headquarters of Les Cartoonistes Dangereux, and we would hold meetings there and use the facilities. We managed to photocopy an entire issue of *Le Roquet* on the Warner Bros.' photocopier that was conveniently placed just outside our office. We used the phones and fax machine, stole art paper and drinks from the bar. I wasn't so much taking the piss, as shoving a catheter down DC's corporate cock and draining its financial bladder dry.

Meanwhile, in my day job, we were putting together a new miniseries, *Millennium Fever*, written by my old friend Nick Abadzis and drawn by Duncan Fegredo. It was going to be the tale of a bi-racial boy, Jerome, and the strange girl he meets and falls in love with. The script had a tenderness and poignancy rarely seen, even in Vertigo comics. It was subtle, funny, sophisticated and had more heart than Hallmark.

Duncan had come down from the frozen North for the day to get some reference photos, as Nick had set the series around South London. The three of us spent the hot summer's day mooching around Putney (that's Putney Bridge in the first issue on page 21, panel 4) taking snaps, discussing the plot and generally having a lovely time. Afterwards, Nick came back to my flat in Notting Hill, we sat on top of the roof with a couple of beers as we watched the sun go down and we discussed life. It was, as Spalding Gray once called them, "a perfect moment." I had no idea how quickly it was all about to turn to shit.

With Helen and Art in the office I felt like a dwarf in a land of giants, both physically and emotionally. They had struck it off very well together and I started thinking that possibly three was a crowd.

Sparks of jealousy? "Indubitably," as Milligan would've indubitably said. It didn't help that I harboured a small crush on her. I fell in love very easily back then. I blame MDMA for opening out my neural receptors and heart.

With hindsight, my relationship with Art was already very intense. We worked nine hours a day together, would have drinks after work, and often spend weekends hanging out together. I slept on his couch more often than not. It was inevitable that sort of intensity would eventually lead to fractiousness. Our excessive road wasn't going to lead to William Blake's "palace of wisdom." This was "in excess," and we were far more likely to be found self-asphyxiated, hung on the back of a hotel room door.

By February 1994, Helen was officially ensconced at DC and the March edition of *Shop Talk* announced, "DC/Vertigo UK welcomes intern Helen Craven. Her responsibilities include scouting out new British talent..." This was a slight in-joke regarding her propensity for spotting gorgeous men in the street.

On my birthday, Art took Helen and I out to lunch at the newly reopened L'Escargot, the exclusive Michelin-starred French restaurant on Greek Street. Champagne was ordered and the total bill topped £300 (closer to £450 in today's money). All courtesy of DC Comics. "We'll just say you were Pete 'n' Grant," said Art, blithely. While this was a lovely present, part of me started to think that this couldn't last. Art had been working the company credit card so hard the smell of melting plastic permeated the office. Accounts were going to suss on at any moment, surely?

Back then I was too loved up to see the writing on the wall. I was freewheeling towards the cliff-edge whilst holding a map up in front of the windscreen. Slowly, however, the atmosphere in the office began to change. Art was spending more social time with

Helen. This was easy for them, as they lived three blocks from each other. They could both ogle the boys of Soho together on a Sunday afternoon. I was being sidelined. Frozen out.

My woeful insecurities were laid bare for all to see. As a child I'd apparently constantly asked my parents "Are they popular? Who's popular? Am I popular?" This was brought to the fore when, at the Warner Brothers' end-of-season softball joke presentations, I was awarded "Best Member of the Team for Talking More Than Jane." But more importantly, it was presented to Tim "Be My Friend" Pilcher. My excessive drug taking only heightened this pathetic neediness, to the point of me being declared an area of outstanding natural arseholishness.

Regardless of my neuroses, Helen was welcomed into the party crowd and introduced to the mind-altering chemicals that had become so beloved of us all. That summer the parties increased in frequency (if possible) and doses went up. I was taking as many as seven or eight Es a night, constantly topping up and riding the wave until 10 or 11 in the morning.

Things were going wrong editorially as well. Titles were slipping and creators were missing deadlines. Art handed me the poison chalice that was *Tattered Banners*. This four-issue miniseries—by Keith Giffen, Alan Grant and Mick McMahon—was a tale of a man out of tune with the universe, aware that something was wrong, but unable to define what. Was this a message to me? The series was something that Art had commissioned back in the Touchmark days. That was three years ago, and all that was completed was half an issue of artwork. Giffen was supposed to be plotting out the story and Grant was supplying the dialogue. The only problem was that the first half of that partnership wasn't delivering. I rang Giffen on an almost daily basis to try and find out where the few pages of plot were. Every time, he would come up with a different excuse. His mother in-law died. His dog died. The computer was broke, etc., etc., etc. Being on the other side of the Atlantic, I had no way of checking the veracity of these excuses, but either Giffen was throwing me curveballs every time, or he was the unluckiest son-of-a-bitch ever to walk the planet. No matter how much I begged, cajoled, threatened or pleaded, I was still lucky to get a page of plot once a fortnight. This was just the basic story outline, mind you, he didn't even have to write the dialogue! And all the while poor Mick McMahon was waiting for pages to draw, unsure whether he could take additional work on in between the long pauses in the script pages without scuppering the schedule. He needn't have worried.

We had the same situation with *Shadow's Fall* by writer John Ney Rieber and artist John Van Fleet. The comic was a dark tale about a man who'd literally become separated from his now sentient shadow, which was terrorising his hometown, driving victims to suicide. Van Fleet was producing some impressive—if overly dark— collage/photographic artwork that, to this day, I don't know how he produced without the use of a computer. But the weakest link was Rieber. He was going through some existential crisis or something and had stopped delivering scripts. Despite both creators living in Chapel Hill, North Carolina, we were having to mediate across the pond as their working relationship broke down. Worse, we'd already published the first four issues of the six issue miniseries, so we were already committed to finishing the project. The story almost became an allegory for that creative process; Rieber, the dark, elusive shadow, driving poor Van Fleet to despair. Eventually we managed to tease a page a day from Rieber over the next few months. Each morning we'd come in the office to find another single page waiting in the fax machine tray. It was like pulling teeth.

And they weren't the only ones. More and more titles seemed to be slipping their schedules. Our partying was starting to affect our workload and relationships.

It all reached a head at a party later that summer at Paul and Ellie's house in Borehamwood. There were the regular gang of comics professionals and Showcase regulars, including Big A, Milligan, and Simon and Annabel Jowett. And, as always, the usual mixture of casual chemicals were to hand: coke, Es, and dope-laced space cakes.

Doug and Sue Braithwaite also attended the party that night and, shunning chemical enhancements, gazed on in bemused horror at the Bacchanalian tableau laid out before them.

Cheeky, my mate from Comic Showcase, ate one of the hash brownies and an hour later felt seriously unwell. Paul asked him which one he'd eaten. "The large one," he replied. "Oh. Oh! That wasn't meant for you! That was for… someone else. I think you better go and lie down upstairs." Poor Cheeky spent the rest of that night tripping out of his head and completely nauseous as he lay on Paul and Ellie's bed, while two unrecognisable, Ecstasy-high men made out next to him. Years later he discovered that the brownie had been meant for me.

It comes to something when your "friends" start spiking you at a party to shut you up. If I'd known that back then, that might have been my wake-up call. As it was I remained blissfully unaware of the entire incident for almost a decade.

You know that arsehole who turns up late at a party, already mashed out their head; who then drinks everyone's booze, breaks glasses, spills red wine on the carpet, fondles your girlfriend and throws up in the washing machine? That was me. I was the father of all dickheads. You could say I was forced to do things. You could say that I was naïve, that I was at an impressionable age. But that would be a lie. The fact is, I suffered from Vertigo. That horrendous feeling of being up high, standing on the ledge, peering down at the long, circular staircase I'd just climbed with trembling legs and a cold sweat on my forehead, like a demented, obsessed Jimmy Stewart. My past spiralling out below me, and my future uncertain. And all the while fighting that lemming-like urge, that demanding, screaming voice inside shouting "Jump! Jump! Jump!"

The atmosphere in the office had become beyond awkward. Art was acting differently. He avoided me as much as possible, rarely speaking, coming in late and leaving early. Actually, he wasn't acting *that* differently. But it was like a couple splitting up. I knew something was up but I couldn't reach him. He wouldn't engage. Was it something I'd said or done? Was I not doing my job properly? Give me something to work with! Truth was I'd become a liability. A loose cannon that was becoming increasingly out of control.

Eventually the fateful hot Spring day came when he asked me to close the office door and sit at his desk. He said my role of "Editorial Assistant" was being made redundant and that what he really needed was an actual "Assistant Editor". I was intrigued at the subtle difference. In reality there wasn't one. It was the only legal loophole Art could use to get rid of me. In my initial contract when I signed on for my six-month probation period it said "Editorial Assistant" however, when I was taken on full-time, the new contract I signed said "Assistant Editor," as did every credit in the books I worked on. He'd even written in the *On The Ledge* column, six month's earlier, "'We' is my assistant editor, Tim Pilcher, and me." I was seething. The blood rushed around my head as I went red and felt faint. After everything we'd been through—all the sex, the drugs, the comics. All the late night heart-to-hearts—this is what I get?

"Oh. So, I guess a certain person's getting my job then?" I said venomously. Art just looked away sheepishly in silence, confirming my suspicions. I didn't blame Helen for getting in there. Actually... at the time I thought she was a conniving cuckoo bitch. But if I'm to be brutally frank, I would've done the same thing. It was a valuable lesson. I know she felt bad afterwards.

As I hadn't been technically employed full-time for more than two years I was legally ineligible for a redundancy payment, but Art managed to wrangle a couple of grand as a pay-off. It was hush money, and like a bitch I took it. I figured, foolishly, "Don't rock the boat. Don't burn those bridges. One day you may get to work for DC again." With hindsight, and the information I had at the time, I should have taken them for a whole pile of cash for wrongful dismissal. The role wasn't being made redundant, they were just hiring someone else in my place. But it was time to move on.

The intensity of the "Deadbeat Club" parties reached a crescendo. Fuelled by MDMA-unleashed libidos, couples were starting to have affairs and the whole gang started to fall apart at the seams. Like some sex cult gone wrong, everything was turning to shit. My "surrogate parents", the hub of all the action, the nucleus that held the group together, split up. There was nothing left for me to cling on to. No reliable harbour or safety net. These were the last days of the lotus-eaters.

Those last few weeks passed in a haze. Art's guilty conscience forced him to be as nice as possible, but I was already a broken man. Morrison's *Flex Mentallo* was the last title I worked on. Ironically, it was the first full-length comic series Frank Quitely (AKA Vincent Deighan) had produced for DC. His first was my last. The only artwork I saw come into the office was the first five pages of pencils from Vin and the first page inked. It was gorgeous, impossibly fine pencil lines, whose delicacy just about clung to the paper. I just had time to tell him how much I loved the art and then I was gone. That was it. A mere 27 months later and the dream was over. The best job I had ever had, or was ever likely to have, had been stripped from me. You could say I was bitter. You could say I was angry. You could even say I was depressed, shocked and deeply betrayed. Truth is I was a little of all those things.

At the height of it all, when we walked into a room the place stopped. Everyone knew who we were, and we were treated like stars. We had it all, and it was all free. Truckloads of swag. Comics, graphic novels, drugs, sex, booze—all for the asking. Our boyfriends, girlfriends, work colleagues, family, everybody rode along. Anything I wanted was only a phone call away. We ran everything. We paid the creators. We paid the dealers. Everybody had their hands out. We walked out laughing. In comics somebody always knows someone, and anything was possible. We were the biggest fish in a small pond. We ate in the best restaurants, drank the finest booze and charged it all back to expenses.

And now that was all over.

I didn't even get to see the first issue of *Millennium Fever* come out. The one series I felt a true affinity with, having worked on it from the very start, and my name doesn't even officially appear in it. However, Duncan snuck in his own credit to me and named the pub in the first issue, "The Tim" in my honour. It was a lovely thing to do, a farewell salute. A comic book "Taps."

I dropped out of comics for a couple of years after that. The whole experience had given me a bad feeling I wanted to shake. After a spectacularly dismal attempt at trying to start a writing career, I managed to blag my way into a job at Penguin Children's Books as their press officer, covering maternity leave. I'd entered "proper" publishing and turned my back on my first love, comics.

I went cold turkey for two whole years. Two years of not buying comics, not visiting comic shops, not going to conventions or meeting up with all my creator friends. Two years before they eventually sucked me back in. I couldn't stay away. I love comics. Always have, always will. After all, I had "four colour funnies" running through my veins before I'd even heard the expression. Cut me and I bled cyan, magenta, yellow and black. I inhaled the musty smell of old comics as if they were perfume. I sweated—well, I'm sure you know the rest.

AFTERWORD

I kept in touch with Art for a while afterwards, still desperately misguided that I may be able to win him back round. I was so desperate to get my job back that I even attempted a clumsy cocaine-induced seduction of Art in his flat, and was rightly rebuffed. But finally the accountants caught up with him and Helen. The comics industry imploded, sales plummeted and DC could no longer justify the lavish London office expenses, so it was shut down and he was called back to New York. But Art's roots were now too firmly planted into British soil. After the freedoms he'd experienced, there was no way he could go back to working under the watchful gaze of Karen again. So he jumped the DC ship for the second, and final, time. He stayed in the UK and got a job at Boxtree publishers, who were dipping their toes into repackaging Marvel graphic novels. I met up with Boxtree's former MD, Adrian Sington, years later and asked him what Art was like as an employee. He simply rolled his eyes.

Art then got a job script editing on *EastEnders*, thanks to our mutual chum, former *Deadline* editor Si Spencer, who was already working on the show. It was the job Art was made for. But that didn't last long either, and he took a succession of decreasing jobs on TV soaps, including the *Crossroads* re-launch on ITV (where he even convinced Milligan to write a few episodes), Channel 4, then 5. Last thing I heard, he was writing soap operas in Russia. Helen felt as bitter as me about the whole experience and left comics for good. Warner Brothers eventually deserted the Wardour street address for offices on the other side of Oxford Street—it's now a restaurant.

Not a single member of the Wardour Office team works at Warner Brothers any more. And for all our tribulations and personal upsets, the comics industry simply rolled on regardless.

For all the highs and lows, it was an incredible and unique experience. If anything could sum it up, it's a line from Ridley Scott's 1982 film, *Bladerunner*: "The light that burns twice as bright burns for half as long." And the Vertigo London office burned so very, very brightly.

Oh, and *Tattered Banners* was not published until 1998, seven years after it was originally commissioned.

KICKSTARTER CREDITS

THIS BOOK WOULD NEVER HAVE EXISTED IF NOT FOR THE FOLLOWING WONDERFUL PEOPLE WHO GAVE THEIR MONEY TO SEE IT HAPPEN:

Kevin Abbott

Arthur C. Adams

Andy Agnew

Ignacio Alcuri

Roly Allen

Aldo Alvarez

Rafael Alves Azevedo

Anonymous (x4)

Gary S. Arkell

Roger Ash

Erico Assis

Rex Banner

Douglass Barre

Simon Belmont

Mark Benjamin

Jason Bergman

Dan Berry

Hannah Berry

Big Bang Comics

Bruno Billion

David Bishop

Stephen R. Bissette

Mark Bowers

Paul Braidford

Stephen Bridge

Jeremy Briggs

Ade Brown (Just1Page)

Jonathan Browne

Jimmy Broxton

Marc Bryant

Matthew Bunce

Stephen Thalarctos Burnside

James Burt

Philip Cahiwat

Liam Christopher Cairney

Laurence Campbell

Stephanie Carey

KC Carlson

Wakefield Carter

Richard Case

Shane Chebsey

Ivan Cherniavski

Cliff Chiang

Aaron Churchill

Theo Clarke

Ian Clarke

Paul Collicutt

Paul Cornell

Ray Cornwall

Stephen Couch

Alan Cowsill

Michael Crouch

Neal Dalton

Dave

Donkey Dave

Christopher Day

Eddie Deighton

Florian Diederichs

Thomas Diener

Jason Doctor

Eugene "Tinman" Doherty

Andrey Dolganov

Matt Donaldson

Cyn Duby

Craig E

Jay Eales

Caroline Earle

Jochen Ecke

Luke Eperthener

Gary Erskine

Tony Esmond

Kate Essam

Garen Ewing

Al Ewing

Andrew Farrell

Ricardo Amaral Filho

Carl Flint

Simon Fraser

Leigh Gallagher

Simon Gane

Jaime Garmendia

Marcus Gipps

Paul Goddard

Gary Gray

Robert Greenberger

Vivian Greene

Sa Greenious

Ken Grobe

Gerard Guero

Gary Halpin

Martin Hand

Jim Hanlon

Ben Harvey

Tim Hayes

Richard Hayes

Peter Hensel

Andy Higgs

David Hine

Kenneth Hite

James Hoare

Peter Hogan

Leon Holden

James Hollywell

Jason Hook

J

Theacpolis Jackson

Martin Jackson

Jeremy

Stephen Jewell

Jo-L from Omaha

Adam Juniper

Gene Kannenberg Jr.

Mark Katzoff

Scott Kelly

James Kennedy

Neil Kenny

Dave King

Jason Klein

Steven D. Kohler

Nikolay Kolev

Hayley Spencer, KomiX

Jonathan Korman

Vincent Kuka

Karin L. Kross

Roger Langridge

Zara Larcombe

Emma Laslett

James Lawrence

Ben Le Foe

Tony Lee

Robin "UKDane" Lees

Jessica Leffier

Johnathan Lewis

Steve Loiaconi

Lombear

Niall John James MacDougall

Vasiliki Machaira

Mike Maddox

Techno Man

Patrick Marcel

Kevin J. "Womzilla" Maroney

Brendan McCarthy

Helen McCarthy

Jamie McCartney

Gordy Mclean

Joe "I sorted Banksie for poppers"

McNally

Joel Meadows

John Medany

Martha Thomases Media Goddess

Rod Meek

Cheeky Joe Melchior

Stephen Mellor

Mike Meltzer

Nathaniel Metcalfe

Jeff Metzner

Nicole Mezzasalma

Mind of Mirrors

Glenn Møane

Justin Mohareb

Michael Molcher

Stuart Moore

Leandro Moreira Duarte

Stephen Morris

Scott Morrison

Greg Morrow
Paul Mounts
David Moyes
Tom Murphy
Joe Murray
Duncan Nimmo
Douglas Noble
Sharyn November
Pádraig Ó Méalóid
Darrin O'Toole
OK Comics
Andy Oliver
Joëlle Oosterlinck
Alex Osbourne
Pat
Andrew Pepoy
Mike Perkins
Carl Petre
Sean Philips
Woodrow Phoenix
Oliver Pickles
Hannah Platt
Wayne E. Popelka
William Potter
Ernesto Priego
Michael "ComicsDC" Rhode
John Riches
Kevin Robinson
Hazel Robinson
Jonny Rocket

Anthony Rooney
Simon Russell
Robyn S
N Savory
Arnaud Savry
Florian Schiffmann
Zach Schlein
Michael Schmidt
Jenni Scott
Joshua Shapel
Richard Sheaf
Drew Shiel
John Simms
Colin Smith
Laura Sneddon
Spacetoast
Gio Spinella
Bob Stahley
Stella Starr
Tristan Stephens
Andrew Stickland
Martin Stiff
Tim Stroup
Sean Sutton
Derek Sykes
Kevin Symonds
Mark Taormino
Ben Thacker
David C. Thompson
Troy Thompson

Nikki Tilbury
Tim
David "The Dude" Timney
Nick Titchener
Marty Trengrove
Andrew Turk
Nick Turner
Cat Vincent
Roland Volz
Jovanka Vuckovic
Stephen Ward
Jessica Watkins
Alan Watson
Darren Watts
Carole Anne Weir
Alex Weir
Julie Weir
Aaron Weller
Geoffrey D. Wessel
Jim Wheelock
Anton Wijs
Charles Wilkins
Chris Williams
Reuben Willmott
Andrew Wilson
Ellie Wilson
Ray Winninger
Jonathan Woodward
Alan M. Wright
Arthur Wyatt

INDEX

Barker, Martin 8
Barker, Richard 20
Barr, Mike W. 21
Bateman, H.M. 62
Bateman, Pippa 41
Bateman, Tim 41
Batman 16, 18, 21-22, 32, 43, 48-49, 74, 80, 89, 92, 114, 119
Batman and the Outsiders 18
Batman: Year One 49
Battle 6-8
Battle Picture Library 11
Beano, The 6, 23, 26
Bennent, Michael 117
Berger, Karen 19, 21, 23, 25, 55, 58, 60, 75, 83, 85, 93, 96
Bill the Clown 83
Birch, Paul H. 61
Bird, Richard 63
Bishop, David 9
Bisley, Simon 53, 56, 59
Bizarre Boys 109, 113
Blaam! 49
Black Orchid 39, 84, 86, 95, 98
Blade II 37
Bladerunner 138
Blake, William 128
Bloom County 31
Blue Beetle 18, 98
Blur 43, 45, 93, 95
Bolland, Brian 5, 10, 12, 17, 19, 21, 38
Bolton, John 21-20, 38, 56, 59, 66
Bolton, Liliana 66
Bond, Philip 1, 44, 88, 94, 108, 113, 125
Bond, Shelly. *See* Roeberg, Shelly
Born Slippy 91
Boswell, David 40
Bough, Frank 8
Boxtree 137
Bradbury, Ray 5

London Cartoon Centre 51, 54
London's Dark 54
Longcroft, Sean 47
Lynch, Bob 47, 58

M.A.C.H. 1 8
Mackenzie, Alan 9
MAD 35
Madonna 98
Mahabharata 94
Mankoff, Robert 75
Marshall Law 42
Martin, Alan 43-44, 92, 94, 115, 120
Martin, Andy 48
Marvel 5, 11-13, 16-18
Marvelman 14
Marvel UK 5, 12-13, 53, 64-65, 68-69
Massey, Lis 14
Mastin, Pete 63
Maus 23
May, Phil 62
Mazzucchelli, David 65
McAlpine, Duncan 35
McCallum, Rob 93
McCarthy, Brendan 19, 21, 23, 25, 29-30, 38-39, 91, 94
McCarthy, Jim 25
McCrea, John 47, 49, 62, 66, 108, 105
McKean, Dave 38-39, 43, 45, 52, 55, 84, 86
McKeever, Ted 38-39, 77-78
McLaughlin, Chris 93
McMahon, Mick 23, 25, 38, 129-130
McNamara, Dave 57
MDMA 1, 105, 109, 111, 117, 122, 128, 133
Meadows, Joel 48, 53, 56
Meadows, Matt 48
Meanwhile... 18, 20, 57
Mega-City Comics 20
Mercy 56, 59